COMPUTERIZATION OF WORKING LIFE

Edited by

E. FOSSUM
Research Fellow
Norwegian Computing Centre

ELLIS HORWOOD LIMITED
Publishers · Chichester

Halsted Press: a division of
JOHN WILEY & SONS
New York · Brisbane · Chichester · Toronto

First published in 1983 by
ELLIS HORWOOD LIMITED
Market Cross House, Cooper Street, Chichester, West Sussex, PO19 1EB, England

The publisher's colophon is reproduced from James Gillison's drawing of the ancient Market Cross, Chichester.

Distributors:

Australia, New Zealand, South-east Asia:
Jacaranda-Wiley Ltd., Jacaranda Press,
JOHN WILEY & SONS INC.,
G.P.O. Box 859, Brisbane, Queensland 40001, Australia

Canada:
JOHN WILEY & SONS CANADA LIMITED
22 Worcester Road, Rexdale, Ontario, Canada.

Europe, Africa:
JOHN WILEY & SONS LIMITED
Baffins Lane, Chichester, West Sussex, England.

North and South America and the rest of the world:
Halsted Press: a division of
JOHN WILEY & SONS
605 Third Avenue, New York, N.Y. 10016, U.S.A.

©1983 Norwegian Computing Centres Research Group/Ellis Horwood Ltd.

British Library Cataloguing in Publication Data
Computerization of working life. –
(Ellis Horwood series on computers and their applications)
1. Labour Supply – Norway   2. Computer – economic aspects – Norway
I. Fossum, Eystein
331.1   HD5800

Library of Congress Card No. 82-23338

ISBN 0-85312-584-8 (Ellis Horwood Ltd., Publishers)
ISBN 0-470-27409-3 (Halsted Press)

Typeset in Press Roman by Ellis Horwood Ltd.
Printed in Great Britain by R. J. Acford, Chichester.

Originally published in Norwegian as *Edb Og Arbeidsliv* by Tanum Norli 1982.

COMPUTERIZATION OF WORKING LIFE

THE ELLIS HORWOOD SERIES IN
COMPUTERS AND THEIR APPLICATIONS

Series Editor: BRIAN MEEK
Director of the Computer Unit, Queen Elizabeth College, University of London.

INTERACTIVE COMPUTER GRAPHICS IN SCIENCE TEACHING
Edited by J. McKENZIE, University College, London, L. ELTON, University of Surrey, R. LEWIS, Chelsea College, London.
INTRODUCTORY ALGOL 68 PROGRAMMING
D. F. BRAILSFORD and A. N. WALKER, University of Nottingham.
GUIDE TO GOOD PROGRAMMING PRACTICE: 2nd Edition
Edited by B. L. MEEK, Queen Elizabeth College, London, P. HEATH, Plymouth Polytechnic, and N. RUSHBY, University of London
CLUSTER ANALYSIS ALGORITHMS: For Data Reduction and Classification of Objects
H. SPÄTH, Professor of Mathematics, Oldenburg University.
DYNAMIC REGRESSION: Theory and Algorithms
L. J. SLATER, Department of Applied Engineering, Cambridge University and H. M. PESARAN, Trinity College, Cambridge
FOUNDATIONS OF PROGRAMMING WITH PASCAL
LAWRIE MOORE, Birkbeck College, London.
PROGRAMMING LANGUAGE STANDARDISATION
Edited by B. L. MEEK, Queen Elizabeth College, London and I. D. HILL, Clinical Research Centre, Harrow.
THE DARTMOUTH TIME SHARING SYSTEM
G. M. BULL, The Hatfield Polytechnic
RECURSIVE FUNCTIONS IN COMPUTER SCIENCE
R. PETER, formerly Eötvos Lorand University of Budapest.
FUNDAMENTALS OF COMPUTER LOGIC
D. HUTCHISON, University of Strathclyde.
THE MICROCHIP AS AN APPROPRIATE TECHNOLOGY
Dr. A. BURNS, The Computing Laboratory, Bradford University
SYSTEMS ANALYSIS AND DESIGN FOR COMPUTER APPLICATION
D. MILLINGTON, University of Strathclyde.
COMPUTING USING BASIC: An Interactive Approach
TONIA COPE, Oxford University Computing Teaching Centre.
RECURSIVE DESCENT COMPILING
A. J. T. DAVIE and R. MORRISON, University of St. Andrews, Scotland.
PROGRAMMING LANGUAGE TRANSLATION
R. E. BERRY, University of Lancaster
MICROCOMPUTERS IN EDUCATION
Edited by I. C. H. SMITH, Queen Elizabeth College, University of London
STRUCTURED PROGRAMMING WITH COMAL
R. ATHERTON, Bulmershe College of Higher Education
PASCAL IMPLEMENTATION: The P4 Compiler and Compiler and Assembler/Interpreter
S. PEMBERTON and M. DANIELS, Brighton Polytechnic
PRINCIPLES OF TEXT PROCESSING
F. N. TESKEY, University of Manchester
ADA: A PROGRAMMER'S CONVERSION COURSE
M. J. STRATFORD-COLLINS, U.S.A.
REAL TIME LANGUAGES
S. YOUNG, UMIST, Manchester
SOFTWARE ENGINEERING
K. GEWALD, G. HAAKE and W. PFADLER, Siemens AG, Munich
INTRODUCTION TO ADA
S. YOUNG, UMIST, Manchester
COMPUTERIZATION OF WORKING LIFE
E. FOSSUM, Norwegian Computing Centre

Table of Contents

TECHNOLOGY AND EMPLOYMENT
Arne Maus

WORKING WITH VISUAL DISPLAY UNITS
Kari Thoresen

Foreword

Alan Burns, Working Environment Research Group,
University of Bradford

Over the last few years, computerized equipment has moved away from being merely a specialist tool to one which impinges upon all members of society. This proliferation of modern technology in the developed nations has been widely publicized and is a result of scientific progress, economic influences and, in many instances, military spending. The impact of these advances has also been the subject of much public debate affecting, as it does, personal privacy, employment levels and the working environment. One group that has studied this latter topic in detail is the Norwegian Computing Centre. Their work is both significant and instructive, not only within the Scandinavian context but for all nations involved with the introduction of new technology, or EDP (electronic data processing) as it used to be known.

In Britain, as with many countries, unemployment has been the major social issue to emerge from the application of new technology. After all the unemployment rate has been, at least previously, an accurate barometer of economic activity. Moreover for most people unemployment is in itself a far more important measure than other national statistics such as gross national product or the inflation rate. But the effect of technical changes on employment is a far more complex subject than the simple analysis of national job levels would indicate. What is of equal significance is the kind of work that will remain for those with employment. Similarly the privacy debate is not just about the use/misuse of personal data but is equally concerned with citizen surveillance and the monitoring of working activity. Only recently have trade unionists, management and academics begun to appreciate the importance both to worker satisfaction and to organizational efficiency of understanding the social role of information technology within the context of the working environment.

By contrast the Norwegian Computing Centre set up its first project in this area in 1971, effectively before the era of microelectronics and certainly before the unemployment issue was raised to public consciousness. This initial work, known as the Iron and Metal Project, concentrated on an educational programme to assist the workforce (and in particular trade union officials) to participate in the planning function of the organizations in which they worked. Training sessions were organized nationally and locally. What is significant about this project is not only the time at which it was undertaken but also the fact that, from the outset the Norwegian Computing Centre saw its role, not as a group of experts representing the workforce, but as a support team. They were a resource that was available, if called upon, to give technical advice to the workforce and its negotiators. In practice therefore they achieved a method of working that many commentators have advocated. For instance Professor Davis of the Quality of Working Life Center at the University of California has stated, in very strong terms, his view that 'no-one has the moral right to design the work and work situation of another person. The role of the expert, whether he be engineer, computer systems designer, line manager or external consultant is to help the worker design his own work situation to assist his own efficiency and job satisfaction needs'.

— The impact of new technology on the working environment can be analysed at two levels. Firstly there is the question of health and safety. In general terms EDP and other automated techniques lead to an increase in the physical wellbeing of the worker (unless concentrated VDU working is involved). There can, however, be a significant increase in stress-related diseases such as depression, hypertension, chronic fatique and heart disease. The reasons for this are complex but relate to increased work pressure, isolation, close monitoring and supervision, the ncecssity to work shifts and a general lack of control over one's working life. This latter point leads on to the second level at which the impact of new technology can be considered. EDP can be designed to achieve democratization at work. In Scandinavia this is known as a Working Life Science, in Britain it has been called Democratic Systems Design. By advocating this approach the Norwegian Computing Centre has not only helped in the drawing up and passing of sympathetic legislation — the Working Environment Act — but has shown that the most effective method of employing EDP, from all standpoints, is when the people who must use the technology, design it.

Since 1971 the Norwegian Computing Centre has been involved in a large number of projects ranging in scope from manufacture and production to office automation. The experience it has gained is therefore vast and is of use to all who are concerned with the introduction into the working environment of new technology. In the USA a number of empirical studies into the social role of computing have been undertaken, the value of the Norwegian work is that their experience comes from actual involvement. Such involvement is not possible with a non-partisan approach. The Centre's research is action-orientated and unmistakably one-sided; their declared purpose is the promotion of the interest of the workforce. This, unfortunately, is a rare approach and therefore makes this book a valuable commentary on over ten years' work. It describes working methods and techniques for describing and modelling EDP systems, reviews past projects and present legislation, and considers office automation and the health hazards from working with VDUs; but most significantly it shows that democratization of the working environment is a viable alternative to yesterday's autocratic structures.

Alan Burns
Bradford, October 1982

Preface

The Norwegian Computing Centre is a research institute established by the Royal Norwegian Council for Scientific and Industrial Research. The Institute's fields for research and development are data technology, quantitative methods and applied data processing. Within applied data processing, a series of research projects concerning EDP and working life have been carried out during the period 1970–81. These projects have in different ways been pioneering work in this field of research. In this book we have presented results and experiences from some of these projects in what is hoped to be more readable form than the research reports usually will be.

The book is a revision of the Norwegian edition. Some sections have been adapted to meet the requirements of the readers not familiar with laws concerning working life and the organization of trade unions in Norway. The trade unions are described in the first part of the article 'The Trade Union Movement, Research and Data Technology', and the laws concerning working environment are described in section 3 of 'Working with visual display units'.

Each article has its own list of references. As much of the research in the field covered by the book has its root and tradition in Scandinavia, it is inevitable that some of the references are only written in a Scandinavian language. We have tried to write the articles so that they can be read independently of this, but we find it correct to include the original title of our sources.

The projects described have been carried out by a number of persons at the institute – both present and former staff. Not all of them have been mentioned as writers in this book, but they are none the less to share the credit for its existence.

The work on the book has been financed by the Norwegian Computing Centre and the writing has been organized as a project. The writers have been the participants and the undersigned the project leader. The participants of the project have been responsible for one article each. Thereafter the individual articles have been examined and discussed jointly.

We would like to thank everybody who in their way has contributed to the publication of the book — trade unions, researchers, secretaries, the publishers and others.

Eystein Fossum
Oslo, July 1982

Introduction

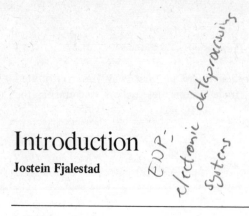

Jostein Fjalestad

1 BACKGROUND

This book contains five articles written by researchers at the Norwegian Computing Centre. The articles, in different ways, reflect various topics connected with a field of research which can only be imprecisely defined as 'the social impact of micro-technology'.

The lively discussion that surrounds the impact of technological development would be a good enough reason for publishing a book of this kind. However, for us, the importance is to give information based on our research activity. At our institute, research has been conducted since 1970 and has gradually been extended to comprise six full-time posts. The development began owing to a collaboration with the Iron and Metal Workers' Union on a project which was to investigate ways in which the union's interests would be affected by the progress of technology, and what strategies would be appropriate to meet this development.

Throughout the 1970s, this and other larger projects carried out for various unions, have formed a major part of our activity. Both the choice of employer, trade union, research method, the orientation towards action research, have to a large degree been understood to be a kind of trademark for our research in this field. This is only partly true. Over the past years employers, research methodology, and orientation have varied considerably. This does not imply a break with our original research traditions, but is a deliberate and necessary supplement.

2 WHAT IS THE SUBJECT OF DISCUSSION?

There is great terminological confusion surrounding the subject of discussion and research that the articles of this book deal with. Electronic data processing is a traditional and well-known term. But lately other terms like 'telematics', 'micro-electronics' or simply 'new technology' have been used more frequently. All these concepts should be relatively easy to define, but they are often used far beyond their original meaning. It is rather doubtful whether this confusion can be eliminated.

Despite this we have to make a choice of terms: 'Computer-based information technology' seems to be the most appropriate. It implies the study of a technological whole, where computers are used in the processing, storing and transmission of information. It also presumes the integration of EDP with other technologies and their adaptation in technical or administrative processes that make up parts of a social system, usually an organization.

The social effects of this integration of technologies and the social system they exist within, vary considerably. The continuing discussion during recent years, has been somewhat limited. A few years ago almost all the attention was focused on privacy. Now it is the question of employment that is receiving attention. Both factors are extremely important, but it is worrying that they have been highlighted at the expense of other equally important topics, such as the working environment. It is in this area that the most significant consequences are in evidence.

Our research has been conducted on a variety of topics, but it is mainly restricted to working life, where the most pressing problems are to be found. But future research should embrace other areas too. For example client relationship, cultural development and the home situation.

3 DEBATE AND RESEARCH: A CONFUSING BEGINNING

Today's discussion on the social impact of technology is marked by conflicting opinions. Certainly, most people agree that the development of new technology based on the use of computers will have far-reaching social consequences. But from this point on, opinions are often contradictory. There are those who picture a society with easy access to information, resulting in democratization and decentralization. Whereas others see a process towards increased control, centralization and less influence on the part of the people affected. There are those who picture a society free from tedious and limiting jobs, as opposed to those who see a process towards the degradation of human labour. There are those who picture a society of economic growth, new job opportunities and more leisure, against those who predict unemployment and social unrest.

Much of the controversy, obviously, stems from politically biased interpretations of the same reality. Yet there is enough disagreement left to show the need for research that can contribute to a better understanding of the possible consequences that can be expected.

When we take a closer look at the variety of opinions, it becomes necessary to make a distinction between research and more general contributions to the debate. In debates, people tend to present arguments and conclusions that are not substantiated by empirical evidence. Certain points may consciously or unconsciously be pushed to extremes. Scientific research must live up to considerably higher standards when it comes to the presentation of evidence and conclusions. This does not imply a devaluation of the public debate on techno-logical development. In a debate one should not be confined to empirical knowl-edge that can be put to the test. There is always room for emphasis, simplification and speculation. The real problem is the blending of debate and research that seems to have taken place over the past few years. Various contributions to the debate claim to be based on more precise knowledge than is the case, and researchers have been presenting work without sufficiently clarifying which parts should be regarded as a mere contribution to the debate.

In principle, however, research and public debate ought to be closely connected. There are times when public debate should be the starting point for research; posing questions and defining problems. At the same time one of the researchers' main tasks should be to feed back information to the public, thereby influencing social development. High standards should be demanded of research so that it does not lose its credibility. Such demands do not imply a return to an old-fashioned belief in absolute objectivity and impartiality in social research.

The close connection with public debate may easily create a series of problems to concrete research projects. Often, research cannot maintain the simplified causal relations and imprecise concepts that are commonly used in the debate. At the same time, in a situation with polarization of the general debate, strengthened by the mass media, research findings are rarely perceived as sensational. This is, partly, because the reality is more complex and varied than is presented in the debate and, also, because it is hard to give unequivocal statements on how the reality will change. The result is that findings may remain unused or, according to the researcher, be misused. He risks being misquoted, and thus has to reject exaggeration of his results by others although he may support essential parts of the messages that his results are fitted into.

4 RESEARCH ON SOCIAL IMPACTS – A DISCIPLINE OR AN ARENA?

One tends to overlook the fact that the main theme of our report is not a recent one. During the 1950s, in the infancy of the computer, there was a heated debate on the social consequences of information technology. It is no wonder that such an invention gave rise to mixed feelings about the future. What is more interesting is the intensity of the debate, particularly with regard to employment prospects, and the remarkable similarity with today's discussion. Two examples:

– Norbert Wiener, one of the pioneers, stated in his book *The Human Use of Human Beings:* 'This (data processing) will produce an employment situation, in comparison with which the present recession and even the depression of the thirties will represent a pleasant joke' (Wiener, 1950). This began a stormy debate on technology and employment which, in the US, resulted in the public report 'Technology and the American Economy'. Norway, also, participated in the debate. Automation and employment was an important issue at the Trade

Union Congress in 1957. As today, the debate was marked by extreme views, 'the optimists' opposing 'the pessimists' and the use of argument was much the same.

⌐Some of the predicted impacts, concerning an increased use of information technology and its effect on the organization of work, are described in an article written by the well-known American sociologist Robert Merton in 1947 (Merton, 1947).⌐ Amongst other things, there is the 'polarization hypothesis', which is so popular today (according to the article it was considered to be a research finding, not a hypothesis).⌐The content is that technical changes, within work organizations, apparently lead to wider differences and larger stratification when it comes to the distribution of qualifications. Since then a multitude of research projects have dealt with the qualification issue.⌐ But these do not seem to have resulted in new hypotheses or findings that differ much.

The similarity between the ideas of past and present is hardly surprising considering the complexity of this technology and its rapid development. What is surprising is that despite extensive research, there still is a substantial lack of knowledge about the social impacts of information technology. In addition, research findings are often contradiciting. A possible explanation can be found in the complexity of the subject; not primarily in the technical sense, but concerning social, economic and cultural aspects. Such research should therefore not be regarded as a united discipline with a coherent basis of theories and methods. It is rather a research arena where the different contributions should be interpreted according to their position within this arena. This also applies when dealing with an apparently well-defined topic (employment, qualifications etc).

A first distinction between different approaches to the arena, is found in the purpose of the research. Is the main objective a synthesis or an analysis? In the first case one wishes knowledge that can be used in the development of new techniques. In the second case the aim is to acquire knowledge about the impact of similar techniques.

There are, of course, also, traditional distinctions rooted in different points of departure with regard to theory, ideology and methods. But owing to the complexity of the arena, it may be particularly difficult to compare the various contributions on such criteria.

A lot of the research topics are typically interdisciplinary. Differences in professional approach will, to a certain extent, determine the way of presenting the problems, the choice of persepctive and methods, and the use of concepts and terminology, thus giving results that may be more or less different. Moreover, researchers that have their professional background limited to a certain sector (as most have) may exceed their powers without really realizing this danger. A typical case is the relationship between social scientists and technologists. The latter tend to be blinded by the speed of technological development and often tend to exaggerate impacts, positive or negative. They lack knowledge from social science for estimating to what extent technology is integrated into the social system, and how social consequences occur. On the other hand social scientists lack sufficient technological insight and therefore tend to understimate the decisive role that technology has. Or they simply fail to understand the subject of research. Therefore, owing to different professional background studies of topics may turn out quite differently and give entirely different results.

[Information technology is not an independent variable behind social change. Rather, it is a means of conveying various interests. Social impact research must therefore be defined and understood on the background of the interests involved.] Research on behalf of the trade union movement, may give different results than research based on the management's approach, although the approaches may be quite similar. In research as elsewhere, reality may be interpreted in various ways depending on whose interests are involved.

The term 'arena' is taken from Kling (1980), who believes that research on social effects is developing into a more uniform discipline. I am sceptical of this attitude. The subject is so complex in its nature that interdisciplinary treatment will always be required. But we have to be more explicit about the premise on which studies are made and pay greater attention to the need for interdisciplinary research. Persons competent in each discipline should cooperate instead of invading each other's professional realm.

5 OUR OWN CONTRIBUTIONS

The previous critical comments will, perhaps, be used in the judgement of our own contributions to this volume. Please note that we do not claim to have found the ultimate truth. Our contributions will be marked by some of the features mentioned.

All five articles are connected with working life. At our institute, most research work falls within this boundary. It is not so much a question of priority, but rather a necessary demarcation line.

Our research on social effects due to the application of computer-based information technology, was initiated by our research for the Norwegian trade union movement. In the first article, *Vidar Keul* describes the content and development of three major projects that constitute a main part of our work in that area. These projects have contributed substantially to our base of knowledge. It has been satisfying working with the projects, both because the work has been closely connected to reality and because the findings seemed to have a direct influence on trade unions and national policy during the process of establishing technology agreements and also in connection with environmental legislation and related regulations.

In short, the main subject of the projects has been 'control' based on knowledge of existing and anticipated impacts of information technology.

In the 1970s work environment, work content and democratization were, supposedly, the most important themes. Employment effects in connection with technological progress did not become a subject for discussion until the end of the 1970s, when it also was adopted on *our* agenda of research.

'Data processing and employment', the most controversial subject of today's discussion, is the topic of the next article which is written by *Arne Maus*. He claims there are reasons to believe that increased use of information technology will lead to increasing unemployment in the years to come. But the causal relationships are complex, which makes it difficult to assess the dimension and nature of the problems.

The importance of potential employment problems as a focus of attention should not be reduced. However, it is evident that this aspect has gradually overshadowed others which are still relevant, like different kinds of environmental impacts. The latter may seem less dramatic and attract less attention, but they represent considerable disadvantages to many workers.

The interplay between the information system, work organization, and work environment is considered a difficult theme, not least when it comes to actual systems design. Our work with systems design is the basis of the next two articles dealing with working environment requirements and modelling or organizations and information systems.

Since the mid-1970s, our institute has been concerned with the interaction between people and computer-based information systems. This is the foundation of *Kari Thoresen's* article about 'Work environment and visual display units'. Unlike other writings on the same subject, the article also pays attention to other than the physical aspects. It is stressed that health and safety problems must be analysed in the light of work organization and psychosocial factors.

It is a complicated task to develop information systems that meet the organization's demand for efficiency and the employees' demands concerning job arrangement and environment, both individually and as a whole. The result depends strongly on what assumptions of how organizations function are used, and how they are translated into descriptions of organizational processes that can be used for the development of computer-based information systems. This constitutes the main theme in *Petter Håndlykken's* 'Description and modelling in EDP systems development'. The article also describes a tool for systems description, the DELTA language, which has been developed at the Norwegian Computing Centre.

Keeping in mind the already mentioned 'arena model', it is worth noticing the inconsistent and varying use of the term 'organization' between these last two articles and the next one. Whereas Håndlykken and Thoresen put their main emphasis on the relation between organization and technology, Pape stresses the relation between organization and society. There are obvious differences in the argument that may be embedded in their original intentions, i.e. synthesis versus analysis, as well as in their professional background, i.e. technology versus social science. The articles seem to confirm that there is room for varying approaches that do not necessarily have to meet with the demands of a uniform discipline.

'The office of the future — some sociological perspectives on office work and office technology' is the title of *Arne Pape's* article. The subject of office automation has gradually attracted attention. Our institute has been working on several projects relating to office work and office technology. This article is an attempt at combining results in this area.

This short presentation of the articles should leave you with the impression that our contributions represent quite different backgrounds and approaches to a large and complex research arena. The choice of themes varies considerably, not mainly because we intended to cover the subject systematically (which we have not done either), but because we let our research experience decide the content. Although each article has been written by a single person, its represents one of several projects in which several persons with different professional backgrounds have been engaged. This interdisciplinary approach has been of great value to our research.

REFERENCES

Kling, Rob, (1980) Social issues and impacts of computing: from arena to discipline, in A. Mowschowitz (ed.): *Human Choice and Computers,* Vol. 2 North Holland Publishing Company, Amsterdam.

Merton, Robert K. (1947) The machine, the worker and the engineer, *Science,* Jan.

Wiener, Norbert, (1950) *The Human Use of Human Beings,* Houghton Mifflin, New York.

The trade union movement, research and data technology

An account of three research assignments for trade unions

Vidar Keul

1 INTRODUCTION

1.1 The trade union projects

In the course of the 1970s, a series of research projects for the trade union movement have been carried out at the Norwegian Computing Centre. Within the scope of this activity are three major research assignments which stand out from the rest, and which usually are referred to as the trade union projects. The projects were organized on similar lines; each of them was assigned by one nationwide trade union, all were financed by public research funds, and they had a methodology and working procedures which in principle did not vary significantly from one project to another.

The three assigning trade unions have the common feature of being among the largest unions within the Norwegian Federation of Trade Unions (LO). Two of them – the Norwegian Union of Iron and Metal Workers (NJMF) and the Norwegian Union of Chemical Industry Workers (NKIF) – organize workers in traditionally important branches of industry. The third union – Commercial and Office Employees' Union (HK) – organizes salaried staff in the wholesale and retail trade and in the manufacturing industries.

All three projects were financed by funds from the Norwegian Council for Scientific and Industrial Research (NTNF). When measuring the work input of the researchers, each project amounted to 3–5 years. The unions on the other hand, were involved through work effort from members and union-elected representatives and in the form of financial contributions to various activities associated with the projects.

The background for the project was the increasing use of EDP which had been observed at the work-places since the early 1970s.

The purpose was to provide the unions with knowledge as to how the use of EDP would affect working conditions and organizations within their respective fields.

Furthermore, the projects were to provide an insight into how members' interests are affected by the introduction of new technology, and how the trade union movement could influence technical change processes within enterprises. Providing knowledge about EDP and working conditions is, therefore, closely linked with the objective of giving the trade union movement improved possibilities of promoting members' interests in this field.

The formulation of objectives and problems distinguishes the trade union projects as action-oriented, one-sided research. In this case, one-sided research implies that the researchers collaborate with one side in the work-place, with the declared purpose of promoting the interests of this party. The projects being action-oriented means on the one hand, that knowledge obtained through research is based on the specific activities undertaken by the unions taking part in the projects. On the other hand, this knowledge is not considered a goal by itself, but is to result in further union activities.

In addition to a common understanding of the nature of the problems examined, there are many features common to the organization and methodology of the projects.

One commonality of all projects is the attention paid to union activity: the trade unionists were to be directly involved in the project work and effect measures on their own. In their work they were to be supported by other parties to the projects – central bodies of the trade unions and the researchers. Such ideas about centrally organized support for activities, directed by local unions and clubs were in the projects associated with experiments with particular methods for project work. In all the projects, local groups were established. These groups were run by local unions taking part in the projects.

In addition to local activities, a series of measures were introduced from central quarters as part of the project work. This included technology reports, inquiries with questionnaires, debates, educational schemes and courses.

Naturally, the actual approaches to the problems dealt with, vary somewhat from one project to another. Moreover, there was a measure of local influence as to what approaches and tasks were accentuated during the period the projects took place. However, all projects come under the same category of problems – the present and future consequences of technological change to the trade union movement. Especially, the projects addressed the question of how the introduction of data processing technology (or EDP) affects the interests and working methods of the trade union movement.

The question of common features of the trade union projects will be more thoroughly discussed in subsequent sections where approaches, methodology and project organization will be treated more in detail (section 5). Before this, parts of the course of events in each of the three projects – Iron and Metal,

Chemical Industry and Commercial and Office Employees – as well as some experiences and results are going to be discussed, these discussions are based on reports from the respective projects (sections 2, 3, 4).

All these sections make allusions to how the Norwegian trade union movement is built up and how it functions. The following discussion of the role of the Norwegian Federation of Trade Unions (LO) may add further clarifications. Additionally, this may serve as a background for understanding possible effects of the trade union projects on Norwegian trade union policies towards new technology (discussed in section 7).

1.2 The Norwegian trade union movement

In Norway there are several trade union associations. The LO is the oldest, the most influential, and the one with the greatest number of members. Founded just before the turn of the century (founding year 1899), the LO forms a substantial part of the organizational basis of the Norwegian labour movement. Traditionally, the two main streams within this movement, the trade unionist and the political, have been rather strongly tied together. The LO has throughout its history maintained close connections with the Norwegian Labour Party. (This party, by orientation social-democratic, continuously formed governments 1935–65, and has returned into government position for shorter periods after that time.)

Organizational basis. Member unions
Through its member unions the LO finds its members among workers, lower-salaried employees within office and commercial occupations and different types of private service work, and large groups of public servants. Workers in manufacturing industries, workers in building and construction, workers in transport, and workers in handicraft-type of work constituted the original basis, and these groups still make up the main part of the total number of LO members. However, following structural changes in the Norwegian economy salaried employees in the private sector and public servants have also been forming their own unions. Some of these unions have joined the LO, gradually constituting a substantial part of its membership basis.

Recently, different groups of public servants have been supplying the majority of new LO members. Among these there are two main groups: employees within different branches of government, and employees in municipal administrations and services. Government employees are organized in various national unions, mostly smaller ones which in matters of common interest (general matters concerning wages, working conditions, co-determination etc.) are acting through their own association within the LO, named the Cartel of Civil Servants. Municipal employees joining LO-affiliated unions are mainly organized in one large nationwide union, the Norwegian Union of Municipal Employees.

The total number of LO members is now 750 000 (overall employment in Norway is 1.9 millions). There are 36 national member unions. The size of the national unions is highly variable: some of them have less than a thousand members, the two largest ones — the Norwegian Union of Municipal Employees and the Norwegian Union of Iron and Metal Workers — have well over 100 000 members.

Principles of organization

The dividing lines between national unions do not reflect one unambiguous principle for the organizational division of the trade union movement. Certainly, the highest ranking authority within LO, the Congress, has repeatedly expressed itself in favour of the establishment of industrial unions, i.e. that everybody employed in a firm should be a member of the same union. Gradually, this principle has become effective with regard to industrial workers. Regarding salaried employees and public servants there are still different principles of unionization to be found. Broadly speaking, by the LO the Norwegian trade union movement is organized according to principles of dividing between industry, between occupations, and between services. The latter is corresponding to principles of unionization within the public sector, although one may find several examples of divisions following occupational lines between unions within the same service. The Commercial and Office Employees Union, the one union of salaried employees which was taking part in the trade union projects at the NCC, may stand as an example of unionization on the basis of a broad occupational criterion. The two other national unions taking part in the research projects which are to be discussed in this article, the Norwegian Union of Iron and Metal Workers and the Norwegian Union of Chemical Industry Workers, are examples of industrial unions. These unions have as their members different categories of workers.

Every national union consists of a number of local unions. In the Norwegian trade union tradition, however, the concept 'local' will have a varying content. The local union may cover one single enterprise, or a number of enterprises, within a geographical area (district, town). In the public sector the unions, as a rule, are formed within an administrative body (branch of government, governmental institution or agency, municipality). In some cases this may make 'local' unions nationwide organizations. (For instance, the Norwegian Union of Government Employees includes a number of nationwide unions organizing civil servants in different government branches.)

Larger unions or unions covering a number of enterprises or departments within an enterprise usually are organized in smaller, more locally based units, named works clubs or groups. The club which constitutes the lowest level in the trade union organization, in many cases acts as an independent organization having its own executive board and shop stewards negotiating and settling agreements with the management at the individual enterprises.

This kind of organizational structure emphasizing the local level constitutes the usual way of building up unions within the private sector. In the public sector the unions are as a rule built up in a more centralized manner, thus reflecting the organizational structure of state and municipal adminstration.

All three trade union projects to be discussed in the following sections were carried out in cooperation with enterprise-based unions or works clubs. This has given the projects a rather distinct orientation towards locally initiated actions or models of action.

A coordinated trade union movement
An important feature of the overall organizational structure of the Norwegian trade union movement is the links between the different unions. So, besides the links to the central LO organization, links are also established at shop and enterprise level and at district level.

In shops or enterprises where the employees are organized in various LO-affiliated unions, particular shop stewards' committees or LO committees may be found. At district level there are local trade-councils. The latter are regular elements within the overall organization, one could say, they are expressing the traditional basic ideas of trade union solidarity and unity across trades and occupations. Except shop stewards' committees at enterprises with a particularly complex union structure which are executing a certain authority and often, do form influential centres of local union work, such joint bodies normally do not play an important part of day-to-day activities.

At the central level, the authority of the LO is distributed between the Congress, normally assembled every fourth year, the General Council which assembles at least once a year, and the Executive Board which as a rule assembles once a week.

Officers elected by the Congress are in charge of the day-to-day work of LO. Cases are also prepared by employed officers. Normally, this staff is recruited within the ranks of experienced shop stewards. However, some of the offices are relying on staff with a professional education, i.e. the Legal Office and the Economics Office. Other offices are the Technical Office which advices national and local unions in questions concerning rationalization and productivity, the Working Environment Office dealing with questions of physical and social nature affecting the working environment, the International Office, etc.

Day-to-day work
The central staff of LO is relatively small compared to the size of the organization. This reflects the division of work between the national unions and the LO and the ordinary procedures, prescribing that the national unions normally should take care of their own business. The officers of LO are expected only to be brought into cases where the unions are not able to reach any agreement with their counterparts, and where assistance is requested by the unions.

Besides acting in internal matters within the trade union organizations and representing the unions *vis-à-vis* their counterparts, the LO officers take part in a great number of publicly appointed bodies (boards, advisory committees, etc.). There trade union representatives meet with representatives of public authorities, of industry associations, and of employer associations; on this occasion, not as opposite parties at the 'negotiation table', but as actors in a collegial type of relationship.

Generally, the work of the trade union bodies is marked by the handling of a great number of incoming cases likely to result in a strain on capacities. Also, this produces a certain working mode which is characterized by a tendency to focus on relatively short-range, problem-solving activities. This may give some indications of why the trade union projects, in spite of the fact that the kind of research work in some aspects was very much like ordinary trade unions' work, could probably not be performed by the unions themselves. (This question is not going to be discussed explicitly, but will be touched upon in some places in the article; see section 7.)

Collective agreements

Wages and working conditions are specified by agreements which may be established at all levels of the trade union organization (shop, enterprise, branch, or sector of economy). Generally, the system of collective agreements is based upon a combination of agreements on different levels. Agreements established at the central level normally will specify certain conditions for agreements negotiated at the local levels. Still, an agreement will not become effective before accepted by vote by the members whom the agreement concerns. By voting, the members also have the right to reject a proposal for a new agreement.

Basic agreements

Mutual rights and obligations, procedures etc. included in the system of collective agreements, are based upon a system of basic agreements. The various basic agreements reflect the structure of the economy and the overall organizational pattern of the Norwegian trade union movement.

Through the LO the unions fall within one of three basic agreements established for each of the main sectors of the economy: the private sector where LO deals with the Norwegian Employers' Confederation; and the two branches of the public sector, the state and the local government or municipal sector. Within the state and local governments the LO members are represented respectively by the Cartel of Civil Servants and the Norwegian Union of Municipal Employees (plus some smaller unions also organizing local government staff).

The system of basic agreements, which viewed by content has many features in common for the three main areas, consists of various parts and a number of additional or special agreements.

One part of the basic agreements specify general rules concerning the right to form organizations and stating the principle of settling disputes by negotiations and agreements. There are also rules concerning the procedures for negotiating agreement, the obligation not to strike during periods of agreements, and procedures guiding the performance of the parties when entering into periods of conflict. In addition, there are separate articles concerning the shop steward system.

Another part of the basic agreements applies to questions of cooperation and codetermination. Generally, the agreements recommend such question to be handled either through the system of shop stewards and negotiations, or by establishing specific cooperative bodies within the enterprises (works councils). Besides handling matters specified in the Basic Agreement, the works councils may also serve as working environment committees which are to be established according to the Working Environment Act of 1977.

The basic agreements are supplemented by a number of additional or special agreements. Within the private sector (signed by LO and the Norwegian Employers' Confederation) there are agreements on the development of work organization; on technological development and computer-based systems (replacing the former General Agreement on Computer-based Systems of 1975, revised 1978); on guidelines for the use of time and motion studies; on equal rights; etc. The Basic Agreement within the state sector includes specific sections on EDP and on personnel policy. Correspondingly, the Basic Agreement within the local government sector also has a specific agreement on EDP as well as on the use of working environment committees.

Basically, the overall system of agreements is having the effect of making a number of problems subject to settling by independent parties, without interference from a 'third party', i.e. the government. Besides, this type of problem-solving and conflict-resolution based upon negotiations and formal agreements imply a rather strong element of local action: Cases should be settled within each company or plant, central bodies should be brought into the process only when local agreement cannot be reached. By specifying general procedures for settling of disputes and by avoiding interference with concrete cases, the role of public authorities supports the principle of independent parties.

State regulation of industrial relations
The Labour Disputes Act contains rules and procedures for settling two kinds of disputes: disputes over interests, and legal disputes.

Regarding disputes over interests, there are rules for the intervention of a mediating authority: the State Mediator may be brought into the negotiations over a new agreement when such negotiations come to a standstill. If the mediation does not bring any results, the process will run into a period of conflict or, eventually, be settled by voluntary or compulsory arbitration. In the latter case it is required that the Norwegian Parliament pass a special act.

Regarding legal disputes, a special court (the Labour Court) has been established by law. If no agreement is reached by negotiations, the parties may continue negotiating before the court. However, if there is no reconciliation, the case will be completed by the court's judgment.

Both concerning disputes over interests and legal disputes, the intervention by the state authorities is based upon, firstly, bringing the parties together to continue negotiations and, in the last instance, settling the disputes by direct regulation by either, law-enforced arbitration or the Labour Court. Usually, it is assumed that the specific modes of state intervention in industrial relations disputes is contributing to creating a pattern of conflict-resolution which is furthering the cooperation between the local parties, having positive effects on the productivity of the Norwegian economy.

Legislation concerning problems of working life

Another aspect of state intervention in working life is demonstrated by the legislation, directly concerning the rights of the employees. The system of negotiations and agreements is supplemented by legislation on two main types of problems: codetermination and working environment. In both cases the legislation has been tied to a strong engagement from the trade union movement.

Following a period of public discussions and experiments during the 1960s, the Parliament in 1972 passed legal reforms concerning industrial democracy. Formally, the reforms are included in certain amendments to the Companies Act. The employees are admitted the right to elect one-third of the representatives of a new managerial body, the Works Assembly, and they are also given the right to have representatives on the executive boards of the companies.

The Works Assembly should be formed in companies with more than 200 employees, while the right of representation from employees on the executive boards also applies to smaller companies. Recently, proposals have been made to introduce a corresponding law-based right of representation for public employees. However, owing to political disagreement concerning how to delimit employee representation in relation to the authorities of parliamentary bodies and of local government, this legislation has been postponed.

The Working Environment Act became effective in 1977. This law which covers both private enterprises and public institutions, is introducing a new set of general objectives and standards for the working environment. Both the physical factors traditionally focused on in legislation on workers' protection, and psychological and social factors are to be considered as relevant aspects of the working environment. The law also specifies the legal basis for an organizational apparatus to handle the whole range of working environment problems. On the one hand there is the Labour Inspectorate, a public authority set up to supervise the implementation of the law. On the other hand, there are the local bodies within the individual enterprises, attended by the working environment representatives elected by the employees. Thus, besides introducing arrangements which should allow the employees to participate in solving their own working environment problems, the law also includes elements of direct state guidance and control. The legislation on working environment matters therefore, imply a certain deviation from the general principles of state regulation of industrial relations.

Trade union policies

Strategic or political questions concerning potential contradictions imbedded in the relationship between the trade union movement and the state authorities, have rarely been considered problematic in relation to the actual policies conducted by the Norwegian trade unions and the LO. Union policies have been built upon an idea that influence can be obtained by a two-way approach: by negotiations and agreements, and by the parliamentary system leading to legislation. The latter approach may lead to general objectives and procedures applying to working life activities and the functioning of the trade union organizations, as well as rules for direct state intervention. Behind these policies, there is the social-democratic tradition which the Norwegian trade union movement represented by the LO has been developing within. This political tradition is contributing to the ambition of combining an independent trade union movement with a relatively strong engagement in working life matters from the state.[†]

2 THE IRON AND METAL PROJECT

The first trade union project is normally referred to as 'The Iron and Metal Project', but the project had a more comprehensive title: The Norwegian Union of Iron and Metal Workers' Research Project on Data Processing, Planning and Control. It was carried out during the period 1971–73.

The Iron and Metal Project had its immediate background in the debate at the national meeting of the Norwegian Union of Iron and Metal Workers in 1970. Here the use of new methods for planning and control was discussed. In this connection, the use of EDP techniques by the individual enterprises was also taken up as a matter for the trade union movement. The discussion particularly referred to a motion tabled at the national meeting, where these questions were raised on a wide basis:

> With reference to the development and use of EDP, the national meeting underlines that active work has to be done with a view to counteracting tendencies towards an establishment of systems where the human being is fitted in as a mechanical and programmed factor of production.

[†] For more detailed information on the LO see: *The Norwegian Federation of Trade Unions* (1978), Published in English by LO, International Office, Oslo.

In cases where the management is not willing to cooperate, the trade union movement must, on its own authority, have the opportunity to carry through reports and studies to strengthen the enterprise, in accordance with the objectives of the employees, and require the management to consider proposals put forward.[†]

On the basis of the resolution made at the national meeting, the union leadership in the NJMF in collaboration with the Norwegian Computing Centre, worked out an application concerning financial support for a research project. Such support was granted by the Norwegian Council for Scientific and Industrial Research, with equivalent amounts for 1971 and 1972, and a lower amount for 1973.

The project was to examine modern planning methods and consider the use of such methods in relation to central purposes of the union's activities concerning working conditions and the management of enterprises. Thus, the project was to provide the basis for considering what demands should be put forward by the union and its members with regard to the use of such methods.

An important aspect was what knowledge the members needed: the project was to examine the need for education at various levels of the trade union movement as regards planning and control within organizations, and to devise a plan for conveying knowledge to the members of the unions. In line with this, the main attention was, during the first period of the project, paid to the making and testing of material for a textbook about EDP and systems for planning and control. The material was presented in the form of a discussion of possible lines of action and strategies for the local union or club.

From the very beginning of the project, the NJMF made it a condition that the project work should be run in collaboration with a group of local unions. As part of the preparations for the project, the central union leadership contacted the workshop clubs at four different enterprises within the machine shop industry. (These were an arms factory also producing computers and control systems, a bicycle factory, a factory producing hydraulic equipment for ships and, a factory producing electric generators.)

However, the activities at the local level were not started until the end of the project period. The plan was for the shop stewards and members of the four clubs to evaluate the educational material prepared as part of the project and take a stand on how the local unions could continue on their own. For instance, if the four clubs were to carry on with the building of knowledge among their members, important questions were what kind of activities were needed for this purpose and how local educational work could be organized.

In practice, it proved difficult for the local unions to get started. Therefore initiative had to be taken by the central project group and, pressure had to

---

[†] The quotations have been taken from the motion carried by the national meeting.

come from the central union leadership before this part of the project plan could be fulfilled.

Once the work began, an encouraging number of members participated. Althogether, 70–80 persons were involved, distributed between three or four working groups in each club.

Experience from the working groups can be read from the reports submitted by the four clubs involved.[†] The work was organized somewhat differently in each club, depending on local conditions. The progress of the work was rather uneven, and sometimes intervention by the researchers was required. Particularly the transition from a phase of study and discussion to a phase of outlining and reporting plans for concrete actions proved difficult to the groups. In some cases the researchers had to take active part in the working groups in order to complete the respective reports. In other cases the groups were able to carry through with their work more by themselves. Generally, reports have to a large extent been written by researchers and discussed with the local unions. Chapters summing up local experience have been written by the groups and local shop stewards.

Materials from the Iron and Metal Project – the textbooks and the local reports – have later been used by the trade union movement, for example in particular courses organized by the Workers' Educational Association (AOF) on 'Planning and Control'. Organizing local union work in accordance with a platform for the planning and control of the union's and club's own activities, has been a central theme in these courses. Such platforms were to be discussed and formulated by the members of the respective unions and clubs. Moreover, the planning of local union work was to be related to a discussion on planning and control of the respective companies, leading to specific 'Company policy action programmes' for the unions and clubs.

Despite such efforts to promote the results of the Iron and Metal Project throughout the trade union movement, there are few examples of unions or clubs actually developing their own programmes according to such a model.

Another proposal for reforms in local trade union work which stems from the Iron and Metal Project, concerns the idea of separate 'data agreements'. This idea has gained acceptability, particularly since the General Agreement on Computer-based Systems was introduced, and gradually became known at the local level of the trade union movement (see the discussion on such agreements in section 7).

The Commercial and Office Employees and the Chemical Industry Projects at the Norwegian Computing Centre continue the model from the Iron and Metal Project. These two projects involve a corresponding set of problems and address similar questions relating to research collaboration with trade unions

† The reports from two of the clubs have been published in connection with the publishing of the textbook from the project. The club reports and the textbook were intended for various educational activities within the trade union movement.

which were generated by the first project. The Iron and Metal Project has also affected corresponding projects in other countries.[†]

3 THE COMMERCIAL AND OFFICE EMPLOYEES PROJECT

The Commercial and Office Employees Project studied the action possibilities of trade unions among salaried staff relating to the introduction of new, computer-based technology. It took place during the period 1976–79.

The project was initiated by the executive board of the union (HK), who in 1974 decided to apply to the NTNF for a substantial sum of money for a research project which was to investigate the impact of new technology on the working conditions of salaried staff. The background to this, stemmed from problems that union members had experienced in connection with the use of computer-based systems. They lacked knowledge about such systems and their potential implications for the firms, the organization of work as well as jobs. In this situation, the shop stewards were uncertain how to act. The problems were presented at union courses where also experience from the Iron and Metal Project had been discussed.

The grant from the NTNF constrained the project to one sector of the union, the wholesale and retail trade. The purpose of the project was twofold. On the one hand, the project was to conduct surveys of the shop stewards' experiences and opinions on the use of computer-based systems in their work, and the types of such systems used in Norwegian wholesale and retail trade. On the other hand, the project was to develop and initiate measures to strengthen the union members' influence on the use of technology. With regard to such measures, the project was to conduct experiments with programmes for education of union members and shop stewards, and working methods for the local unions.

Initially, the project conducted a survey with questionnaires which included all enterprises where the trade union had a wage agreement and more than ten members, i.e. not only the wholesale and retail trade. This study was made to get an impression of the extent of adoption of computer technology at workplaces within the overall field of organization of the Commercial and Office Employees' Union. In addition, a picture was needed of whether and how questions concerning technology were discussed in the local unions: were such discussions frequent, and if so, what questions were discussed? These inquiries also attempted to establish how the enterprises proceeded with the introduction of technology, particularly with regard to the provisions of agreements concerning participation and codetermination from employees and union representatives. Moreover, the questionnaire included a question about suggestions for measures to strengthen the union members' influence on the use of computer technology.

[†] The DUE Project in Denmark and the DEMOS Project in Sweden are incorporating ideas from the Iron and Metal Project. Sandberg (1979) contains articles presenting the DUE and DEMOS as well as the Iron and Metal Projects. For a presentation of the Iron and Metal Project, see also Nygaard and Bergo (1975) and Nygaard (1977).

The inquiry was divided into two parts. As a follow-up to the survey, various steps were taken with a view to feeding back information to the members and contributing to discussions on the survey results at various levels in the union. At the same time, such discussions would allow the correction of misinterpretations resulting from the answers to the questionnaires.

The survey indicated a lack of cooperation between the parties in the enterprises as regards the use of new technology. It was also established that the local unions for their part, wanted to cooperate, and that the shop stewards regarded the technology questions to be of such importance that further efforts in this field was necessary to increase union influence.

Working methods that had been tested in the Iron and Metal Project, served as a model for the work-place experiments in the Commercial and Office Employees Project. Working groups were established at four enterprises within the wholesale and retail trade. The purpose of these groups was to start accumlating knowledge about the impacts of computer systems and clarify possible lines of action for the local unions. The groups were intended to work as agents to initiate such processes†

Experience with local working groups in the Commercial and Office Employees Project compared to the Iron and Metal Project, allow an evaluation of the appropriateness of this method. The specific conditions relating to the field of the Commercial and Office Employees' Union seem to emphasize some underlying problems.

First of all, to conduct the group work according to the plan seemed to involve greater difficulties with Commercial and Office Employees than with Iron and Metal: only one of the groups in the Commercial and Office Employees Project developed the way it was planned. These differences in the course of the project work may indicate that the implementation of the method relies on a more firmly established union organization structure.

Besides, the working method is based on the premise that action will result from knowledge. The problem of this condition is that a clarification of the interests of the union is required. In some cases, the interests may not be understood by the members or, contradictory opinions on what constitutes the 'interests of the union' may appear. In addition, the members may be uncertain regarding what rights and opportunities they have in order to advance their interests within the individual enterprises. Because the model has been developed within Iron and Metal, it may be that conditions which are not present in other unions are included; probably it has been more common in Iron and Metal than in Commercial and Office Employees to build union solidarity from interests which were commonly known and accepted among the members, and to base the work on established methods of action.

---

† The working groups covered: the central wholesale branch of the Norwegian consumers' cooperation as well as its largest local cooperative society; the Norwegian branch of a mutlinational enterprise distributing furniture; and the central department of a nationwide kiosk chain.

Another difficulty relating to the working groups method, is its local perspective. In Iron and Metal it was probably easier to restrict the scope of the problem 'field', i.e. computer-based systems, to the individual enterprise, so that the field corresponds to the methods of action immediately available to the local union. For instance, the investigation of EDP systems in the wholesale and retail trade, which was conducted as part of the Commercial and Office Employees Project, showed a correlation between the introduction of new technology and structural changes in the industry. One aspect of this is the way technology is used, tending to promote a centralization of decision-making. The question as to what are the interests of the union members in relation to such structural changes, cannot sufficiently be answered by local working groups at the individual enterprises. Because the problem field involves questions concerning the overall structure of the industry as well as the adopting of new systems by the individual enterprises, a clarification of interests is needed both at the central and local level. Correspondingly, confronted with such problems methods of local union action will have a lack of efficiency.

The educational strategy in the Commercial and Office Employees Project, was also based on ideas from the previous project. The educational aim formulated in the Iron and Metal Project, was to build knowledge with a view to considering technology and control systems in relation to the objectives of the trade union movement and the members' personal experience. Moreover, the education was to be based on personal activity from the unionists. During the Commercial and Office Employees Project, educational material and courses were arranged with an eye to such principles. In order to avoid keeping the educational programmes of the project off the union's regular activites, one also wanted to make the education fit in with the union's traditional courses.[†]

4 THE CHEMICAL INDUSTRY PROJECT

'The Trade Union Movement and EDP in the Process Industries' project was carried out during the period 1977–80. In this project the Norwegian Union of Chemical Industry Workers (NKIF) engaged two research institutes: the Norwegian Computing Centre and the Institute for Social Research in Industry (IFIM) at the Norwegian Technical University in Trondheim.

In the application from the union to the Norwegian Council for Scientific

---

[†] A separate report from the Commercial and Office Employees Project discusses the experiences with the educational experiments. Other reports from the project include: a report on the survey on shop stewards' experiences with computer-based systems; a report on the EDP systems actually used in the wholesale and retail trade; and a report on the experiences with the working groups. All of these reports as well as substantial parts of the separate working group reports, are written by the researchers taking part in the project. In addition, there is a report written by a member of the central union leadership summing up the results from the project and also discussing its implications for union policies. All reports are published by the Commercial and Office Employees' Union.

and Industrial Research, concerning financial support for a research project on EDP in the process industries, the purpose of the project was defined as follows:

> The project is to give the NKIF and its members a basis for an independent judgment as to how computer-based control systems in the process industries may contribute to promoting their interests in the future, and how existing and proposed systems will affect these interests. Such a basis is necessary for the NKIF and its local unions to be able to carry joint responsibility for and contribute to the development and introduction of such systems.

The NKIF took up a series of aspects of the EDP systems which the union wanted to throw light upon, as regards the way such systems were used in the process industries. The questions included possible impacts of computer-based control systems on the operators' physical, social and psychological working environment, and the influence of such systems on the supply and character of jobs to be found in the enterprises. In this connection, the NKIF wanted to examine the relations between new systems for production control and the possibilities for developing active solidarity among the members. Such solidarity, built on cooperation and social contact in order to solve production tasks, was by the NKIF considered an important condition for obtaining working-life democracy. The union was also interested in having illuminated how new technology could affect the industry, like the overall enterprise structure, the use of raw materials as well as choice of products by the enterprises. Moreover, one wanted to examine conditions for control by society of the technical change processes at the work-places.

The way the project was initially outlined, there were two main elements. On the one hand, the project was to contribute to mapping out and analysing the field of problems, i.e. the questions how EDP systems in the process industries could influence union members' interests as regards working environment, organization of work, supply of jobs, the actual content of these jobs, enterprise structure etc. On the other hand, the project was to be an element in the development of the union's technological policy by providing knowledge upon which policies as well as concrete demands could be advanced by the union and its local branches.

By the Chemical Industry Project, certain approaches to the problem field were emphasized, which made it differ somewhat from the other trade union projects. The Chemical Industry Project was to analyse characteristics of the EDP systems and relations between such systems and various aspects of the conditions of work of process operators. The other trade union projects put less emphasis on analyses and more on participation, by introducing certain experimental activities with a particular view to establishing working methods to strengthen the local union. Regarding the action possibilities of the trade union movement towards the processes of technological change, the Chemical Industry Project in particular also stressed the need for developing policies at the central level.

The Chemical Industry Project was the last in the series of three trade union projects, and the above-mentioned differences in approach could give us reasons to believe that a shift in research perspectives and attitudes to the problems has taken place. There is, however, the question of how much attention should be paid to possible differences in the formulation of specific project purposes. Trying to assess the importance of such differences, the various common features of these three trade union projects should be kept in mind. The Chemical Industry Project resembles the previous projects with regard to central methodological aspects, project organization as well as statements of the overall research objectives.

In the Chemical Industry Project too, local working groups (by this project named 'base groups') were established. Thereby trade unions at three enterprises were directly involved in the project.[†]

In addition to the base groups, another working method based on local activities was introduced by the Chemical Industry Project. A series of meetings were held, where union delegates from a group of four enterprises (all belonging to the ferrosilicon industry and being situated within one geographical region) met researchers at so-called working seminars. The meetings had a similar purpose as the base groups in that the participants, jointly, were to describe their own working situation and whether and how it was affected by technological changes. Moreover, they were to discuss and assess such changes and indicate how the unions could make their own demands as well as how to get organized in order to advance such demands.

While the aim of the research in the base groups was to work out and communicate new knowledge in the trade unions, the working seminars were basically intended as an instrument for exchange of experience and for mutually supporting each others' activities. The meetings should serve as part of a local network which was to ensure the communication of experience and concrete examples of action and encourage cooperation between unions at different enterprises.

Regarding the involvement of union members and local unions, the Chemical Industry Project was to focus on two central elements, i.e. participation and action. The first one, the participation element, seemed to work in a satisfactory way. For example, local activities were completed without the researchers having to assume too much responsibility.

This experience indicates that the trade unions can be able to increase their own capacity when meeting new technology. The base groups and the working seminars illustrated how the unions could overcome a capacity problem by firstly, acknowledging new technology constituting an important field of union activity, and then, by giving the participants opportunities to analyse change processes by means of personal experience from their work-places. Nevertheless,

[†] The three enterprises all belonged to the metallurgical industry, which is the industry having the largest proportion of NKIF members. Working groups were established at two aluminium and one nickel works.

the researchers who took part in the project, doubted the general usefulness of such models. It appears, that some aspects of the base groups' work, for instance, the making of reports, is difficult to combine with local union work.

The second element, the action element, seemed to recede into the background during the project. This could be connected with another general problem met within this type of project work. This problem, has not primarily to do with the working methods as such, but with the integration of the studying and report work with the executive element of the union activity represented by the local union leadership. It appears, that the base groups tend to run their own business outside the current work of the union leadership, which neither will be much influenced by what is done in the groups.

General problems illustrated by the Chemical Industry Project, are: on the one hand, for the unions to become aware and obtaining knowledge of a problem is a time-consuming process; on the other hand, this process does not necessarily result in action. The importance of the local activities in the project is first of all to show what work is required before the unions can develop their own technological policy.

Another point where the project failed to work according to the intentions, had to do with the expected spreading of local activities. During the project, there were contacts with quite a number of unions. Many of them were interested in joining, but the researchers did not succeed in establishing base groups at other enterprises than the three mentioned. The lack of spreading can be explained by the actual experiences made by the groups which did start and, by difficulties met with during the project work.

A principal factor may be that the project was too ambitious in relation to the resources available for the project work and in relation to the importance of the problem in the eyes of the union members. This has to do with the fact that the question of technological change, and particularly EDP, has been a new area which has received relatively little attention from the trade unions. Another explanation is associated with practical difficulties which the participants often came across — such as problems with time, for example, because of shift work etc. Practical obstacles encountered by the base groups thereby illustrate a general problem in union work: it is difficult to organize the activities with regard to the recruiting of active members. Put another way, union work can be performed at a varying degree of involvement from the members.

In the Chemical Industry Project one tried, like the other projects, to engage members by means of various kinds of educational activities. From this part of project work can be inferred that taking part in a course etc. does not necessarily promote activity, which was the general impression from all three projects. The trade union projects have thus emphasized the importance of a local environment which inspires learning and provides opportunities for alternating between the acquiring of theoretical knowledge and the using of concepts and strategies in current union work.

Like the previous projects, the Chemical Industry Project also included a series of activities carried out centrally, by the researchers and the project group.[†] Some of these were intended as a kind of direct support to local activities, for example by education (two one-week courses as well as a series of weekend courses were held), and by debates where all local unions in the NKIF were invited to take part. When considering the overall number of local unions, there were few unions that went through with the debate arrangements. However, the materials actually resulting from this activity, represented a great part of the NKIF members and unions which are most affected by new technology.

Another activity carried out by the central project group is a report made on new technology in the process industries. The purpose of the report was to examine impacts of technical changes on enterprises and the organization of work-places. In particular, the aim was to inquire into what kind of experiences were made by the employees regarding the opportunities to participate when such changes take place. As part of the work with the report, a questionnaire was sent to every local union in the NKIF. The answers that were collected from this inquiry and from the above-mentioned debates, add up to an impression of how the members had experienced the introduction of new technology.

One of the conclusions to be drawn, is that new technology in connection with process automation has contributed considerably to the improvement of the physical working environment. Concerning the social and psychological aspects of the working environment, there were more varying experiences. Many answers expressed the opinion that mental strain had increased, partly as a result of reduced manning and fewer opportunities for contact with fellow workers, and also because of increased supervision of the individual operator's work effort. Other answers stressed that the job has become more monotonous, and that less knowledge and comprehension was required. On the other hand, there were answers pointing to new technology being a source of more challenging and developing tasks and giving better opportunities for surveying the production process.

On the whole, the various investigations in the Chemical Industry Project illustrate a series of contexts where new technology is an integral part. All investigations point to the crucial importance of such contexts, i.e. the technology 'by itself' is not as much the cause of the impacts experienced at the work-places. So, materials from the Chemical Industry Project, both from the base groups and the inquiries, do not allow definite conclusions about the impacts of new technology on the working conditions in the process industries. The impact depends on properties of the technology, which systems are in question, what purposes the systems are to serve etc. For instance, materials from the project show that new technology generally is used as an element of a rationalization process, which either results in an absolute reduction in employees, or relative

[†] See section 5.3, which outlines the model for project organization.

to the production volume. Moreover, the impact will depend on the organization of work, for example the division of tasks into shift and day work.

A particular aspect of the introduction of new technology, concerns possible changes with regard to the qualifications required for the jobs. Generally, such changes can result from more specialized tasks and demands for new skills related to the operation of the systems. On the whole, the new technology seems to require more formal education from new employees. Therefore, experience and knowledge acquired by the already employed could become useless. Such effects are, next, dependent on how the work with new technology is organized, and what opportunities for further training and developing of occupational ability are available. The Chemical Industry Project illustrates that these problems could be met in various ways at the different work-places.

A problem which was clearly expressed, for example by the answers from the debates, was that the union members had too little opportunity to participate during the introduction of new technology. Mainly, this was due to the planning and decision-making processes related to technological changes. The character of such processes prevented the unions from being sufficiently informed and besides, decisions were made in bodies where the unions were not represented or otherwise had no influence.

On the other hand, participation from the union members is depending on their knowledge of the new technology. Participation is also relying on the union's way of organizing their own activity. By the answers from the debates, the need for new channels to promote the employees' interests was emphasized. In particular, local 'data agreements' and 'data shop stewards' were mentioned. (See the discussion on such innovations in union working methods, section 7).

The technology report concerning the process industries, and the remaining project work was to provide the NKIF with a base for drafting the union's technological policy. The results from the research project have been pursued in the 'Technological Programme' which was carried at the NKIF's national meeting in 1980.[†]

5 THE RESEARCH MODEL IN THE TRADE UNION PROJECTS

In the previous chapters the three trade union projects have been treated separately. This chapter will go somewhat further into the research model of the projects. The point of departure is the many similarities between the three projects – Iron and Metal, Commercial and Office Employees, and Chemical Industry. Therefore, they will all be treated as one approach (research model or research strategy) to the actual problem field. Regarding what characterizes the approach of the projects, four criteria are going to be discussed: interests

---

[†] Besides the above-mentioned technology report, there are a concluding report and reports from the three working groups, all published by the institutes responsible for the various parts of the Chemical Industry Project. In addition, the debate and the report on the answers from the debate has been published by the NKIF and the Workers' Educational Association.

orientation, definition of results, project organization, and working methods. This discussion could also give some content to the term 'one-sided, action-oriented' research, often used to distinguish the trade union projects as well as related research.

5.1 Interest orientation

The trade union projects have been based on the condition that they are to serve certain interests. By itself, this condition is not sufficient to give these projects, as research, a distinctive stamp. All research can be regarded as activity to serve one interest or another – there is at least the common feature that research is to serve the purpose of knowledge. What particularly distinguishes the trade union projects from much other research, is the association with certain social interests, defined by the project assignment.

On the other hand, much of the so-called applied research, goal-oriented research, product or organization development work etc. will have the common characteristic with the trade union projects that the activities are based on a defined set of interests. To examine possible distinctive marks of the trade union projects, we have to ask what interests are in question, or what is the relationship between the research work and actual social interests.

To promote the interests of organized labour was an underlying condition for the trade union projects' investigations of change processes in different industries associated with the introduction of EDP. Such explicit interest orientation was to be reflected by the research model, both pertaining to the relationship between the project and the union as a whole, and to the project activities at the individual enterprises. Trends dominating much of research policy by the time the projects were started, explain why this model represented a kind of pioneering work at the beginning of the 1970s. By launching the projects, the Norwegian trade union movement attempted at taking a more active part in research politics and, the institutes as well as the individual researchers were given opportunities for putting the 'one-sided' research model into practice.

The term 'one-sided research' imply the possibility for conflicting interests regarding the actual problem field. However, it is well worth noticing that statements establishing project purposes are relating these purposes to the interests of the enterprise or, the industry as a whole, i.e. the trade union projects are considered as efforts contributing to the enterprise's or the industry's policy towards new technology. One-sided research therefore imply explicit and active identification with organized labour, as well as involvement in discussions to clarify objectives of union policy towards technical change processes, but not necessarily the assumption of conflicting objectives with regard to enterprises or industries (see the quotation from the Iron and Metal Project, section 2).

5.2 How to define results

In principle, the purpose of research is to gain knowledge, without considering the possibilities of applying the knowledge. In the light of this general definition, research to find solutions to concrete problems forms a particular case. The trade union projects have been oriented towards application, and at the same time, they differ somewhat from traditional models for applied research because the primary aim of these projects was not to come up with documented 'solutions'.

The projects have been founded on a definition of the results of the research as *action*; i.e. the projects were to build up resources in order to increase the unions' capability of acting.[†] Therefore, the projects have been emphasizing the instrumental aspect of knowledge. The research work was to give insight into the relation between specific interests and the possibilities of acting in a particular situation.

Such demands made on research work as well as the resulting knowledge can by themselves be regarded results from the trade union projects. Concepts that afterwards appear as central, had not been established in advance, but occurred during the project work. For instance, the first project – the Iron and Metal Project – was originally planned in a more traditional way, based on the collection of information by survey methods and the analysis of such 'data' by the researchers (Nygaard, 1977).

5.3 Project organization

For all projects, steering groups were appointed with a majority of members from the trade union movement, i.e. from the respective unions and from central bodies of the Norwegian Federation of Trade Unions. In addition to the local working groups, there were also central project groups which consisted of researchers and union representatives from the central union leadership and local unions. In this model, so far, there is little that distinguishes the projects from ordinary research assignments. What is non-traditional, is the fact that trade unions have been acting as the assigning part.

The attention paid to establishing good contact with local unions to engage union members in current project work, also contributed to distinguishing the projects from the usual models for research assignments. This gave the specific model for collaboration in the projects between researchers and users of research a trilateral character: the researchers were to have contact and take part in cooperative work at two levels of the union, centrally and locally.

However, the project organization outlined above, does not tell much of what actually was to take place during the project work. In fact, the role which the researchers were to play, varied somewhat from one project to another. The project reports indicate several types of tasks undertaken by the researchers,

---

[†] The original definition of the results from the trade union projects is to be found in the Iron and Metal Project: 'Results are all actions carried out by the NJMF, centrally or locally, which supported by the project, aim at giving the union and its members greater influence with regard to EDP and the managing of the enterprise'. The other two projects – Commercial and Office Employees and Chemical Industry – both refer to this definition.

like taking part in discussions with local unions and the working groups, functioning as advisers to the unions in technical matters, teaching and being course supervisors, in some cases taking an initiative to prevent the local project work from reaching a deadlock, etc. By all appearances, the projects thus have furnished valuable experiences on which such cooperative research model can be built.

5.4 Working methods and activities in the project work

The intended instrumental character of knowledge was to affect the working methods to be applied within the trade union projects. For instance, attempts were made at changing the traditional division of work between researchers and users of research, where the users give information (data) and receive the results worked out by the researchers. In the trade union projects, it was considered important to get union members take an active part in the research process. Such a changed user role also presupposes a changed researcher role. This is most clearly expressed concerning the local working groups. On these premises, the working groups were to choose their own approach to the problems and their own tasks within the main theme of the project. The groups were also to direct their own activities. The researchers' task in relation to the groups, was generally, to function as resource persons and more specially, as advisers in technical matters.

The working groups as well as some other methods and activities were intended attempts at practising a non-professional, non-specialist approach to the development of knowledge. This was considered necessary to obtain the particular results from the projects, i.e. the close interaction between the acquiring and application of knowledge by the unions themselves. In a wider perspective, the approach as well as the specific working methods should contribute to the building of self-supported learning and action processes within the trade union movement.

Project activities can be divided according to the level of project organization on which the activities take place. Below, the working methods and activities within the trade union projects are discussed in three parts, the local, the central, and the local-central activities.[†]

Local activities

Local activities were centred on the working groups. In each project, such groups were established at three to four local unions. As a method for project work, these groups — which are referred to by various terms like working groups, base groups, study groups — show a series of characteristics. The following survey will to a certain extent give an impression.

(1) The groups were estabilished as parts of the project work in the way that tasks, objectives, time limits etc. for the group work were determined on the

† This division corresponds to a summary of methods and activities presented by the Chemical Industry Project.

basis of the overall approach and the work schedule of the project. Within this framework, the groups could, in consultation with the researchers and central bodies of the union, choose which tasks to carry on with.

(2) The groups were based at individual enterprises and were run by the local unions which took part in the project. The group members were recruited among shop stewards and ordinary members.

(3) The groups consisted of relatively few persons. In all three projects, the number of group members varied between three to four and eight to ten members. In addition, one or more researchers normally took part in the groups.

(4) The groups expressed an initiative from the part of the employees – as opposed to project groups, cooperation committees etc. with representation from all parties. However, the work was run with the enterprise management's consent, although it was not necessarily formally agreed upon.

(5) To get down to concrete approaches within the main theme – experiences with technical change within enterprises – the groups used a method which is usually termed work-place descriptions. Basically, it implies that the group members, individually or jointly, describe their own working situation and how it has changed due to changes, reorganizations etc. The materials and the opinions brought forward, were to be the starting point of discussing the actual relation between the use of technology in the enterprises and the trade unions' interests.

(6) In most cases, the group work concluded in a report, written by the group members. The idea behind this, was to decentralize also the part of the research work which consists in recapitulating results and presenting them in a written form. At the same time, one also wished to make the reports more easily accessible to the readers, first of all to members of the respective unions. The reports varied in content and size although they mainly were arranged according to the same pattern. They contain a descriptive part and a part where a programme is formulated. The descriptive part is based on descriptions of the work-places, which were attempted elaborated into more complete descriptions, including descriptions of the enterprises, the use of technology, as well as the union's position and relevant union interests. In the part formulating the programme, measures are proposed which can be instituted and directed by the union.

Summing up, the working groups represented an attempt at combining elements of the project work from the local and the central levels. This was to be done in such a way that the main emphasis was put on local work, yet as part of a project plan which was designed by central project groups. The groups were set up with a view to activating the members and opening for local initiatives and local experiences. Moreover, the group work was intended as a method of attaining knowledge by letting union members work with their own experiences, supported by researchers who could supply different types of general knowledge, i.e. insight into technical questions, questions relating to the organization of work, project work, etc.

The groups met with difficulties of various kind during their work. Recruiting people for the groups sometimes was difficult as well as finding a suitable approach to the problems. Furthermore, a lack of time and varying interests and motivation among the group members hampered the carrying out of the group work. Thereby the groups had varying success with fulfilling the original intention of their work. In some cases the researchers had to assume greater responsibility for the group work and the writing of the final report than was planned.

Central activities

The trade union projects included a series of activities directed at the central level. Common to all projects are two types of activities.

On the one hand, there are analyses of the technical change processes affecting enterprises within the respective industries. In the last two projects, the analyses of new technology and its implications were restricted to respectively, the wholesale and retail trade, and the process industries. The Iron and Metal Project dealt with EDP generally, in systems for planning and control of work.

The second category covers various educational activities. These include working out programs, courses etc. as well as organizing and carrying through such plans.

Local-central activities

The category involving both two levels in the project organization (central, local), covers various activities at different stages of the projects. A division can be made, for example, between an introductory phase of contact and search, an intermediate phase characterized by attempts at activating local bodies of the organization, and a phase of spreading also intended to continue after the project has been completed. Examples of activities which took place in the introductory phase are visits to local unions, meetings with local union representatives, the selection of unions willing to start local working groups. Activities in the intermediate phase of activation, varied somewhat from one project to the other and comprised activities like inquiries (Commercial and Office Employees, Chemical Industry), debates (Chemical Industry), local and central courses and conferences (all projects). The phase of spreading involved the presentation of reports, further testing of educational programmes etc. By means of such measures, a larger proportion of the union members was to be engaged than could be involved in the local working groups. Besides aiming at activation, activities like debates, inquiries etc. were intended as channels for discussions and the mediating of information, opinions and attitudes between different levels of the union.

Obviously, the above division of activities and methods in the trade union projects should not be considered a clear-cut and absolute division. For instance, according to the three-part division, the working groups were characterized as a typically local activity. Nevertheless, we may ask how valid this is, when considering the fact that this method, the way it was practised in the trade union projects, basically was planned and initiated from the central level. Moreover, the carrying out of the group work was to require substantial follow-up and support from the part of the researchers. The amount of support and the actual role of the researchers in relation to the groups, varied from one project to another and from one group to another.

In addition to the three categories local, central and local-central, another type of activity can be defined, the local-local activities. Such activities had to do with attempts at establishing direct contact between different local unions to release processes of mutual support. The ideas were tried out in activities like working seminars for delegates from several enterprises, intended to contribute to the forming of a cooperative network.

Especially, when planning the Chemical Industry Project, local-local activities were considered an opportunity to initiate self-supported processes of spreading on the basis of the project. However, such activities were to play a minor part of the actual project work.

5.5 Similarities and dissimilarities in the project design

By the discussion on the approaches of the trade union projects, the three projects are presented as variants of one research model. Named by the first project, this model has often been termed the Iron and Metal model.

A central element of the model is local *action*. Action is considered an integral part of the overall process of union work. On the one hand, action is built on the union members' experiences and more systematically worked out descriptions and analyses. On the other hand, action is built on an interpretation of aims and interests which possibly could be changed during the process. The model presupposes that new insight is created as a result of action, and possibly, new working methods for the unions are also introduced. In other words, knowledge, methods as well as organization can be regarded resources created during this process. Such resources are essential in order to change the power structure in the enterprises and thereby influence the introduction and use of new technology.[†]

[†] Variants of an action model, of which the essential features are indicated, have been more thoroughly dealt with in reports from the various projects. In the Iron and Metal Project, the model is discussed on the basis of 'examples of action' and 'cycles of action' in union work. The Commercial and Office Employees Project presents a corresponding action-oriented model based on local union work defined as 'problem solution' on the basis of 'problem understanding'. In the concluding report from the Chemical Industry Project, a model of action is discussed in relation to the unions' 'action resources', based on the unions' acknowledgement of EDP as a 'problem'.

The common research approach was applied at enterprises and industries that have many similar features, for example pertaining to the organization of the unions. The three trade unions have basically the same structure based on local unions which in principle are independent organizations. This structure is reflected in the model of union work incorporated by the projects.

However, it is important to realize differences between the industries, differences that also have affected the course of events in the trade union projects. There are, for example, differences related to industry structure which lead to different uses of computer-based systems. The 'impacts' of EDP thereby would vary from one industry to another. Neither is there the same degree of consciousness about union work in different unions, i.e. consciousness about problems and tasks and what measures and opportunities for acting that are at hand.

All this explains the various outcomes of the trade union projects. Differencs occur, partly because the industries or the fields of research, are dissimilar, and partly because, in practice, the approaches were varied somewhat in order to be adapted to the conditions underlying the work of the individual unions. This also shows that it is relevant to ask in what way and to what extent action-oriented research models can be transferred from one sector of society to another.

6   RESEARCH POLICY AND RELATED RESEARCH

6.1   Attempts at a professional reorientation. Research policy implications

In line with their main purpose, the trade union projects aimed at establishing a direct dialogue between the professional project workers (a varying number of researchers were engaged at different stages of project work) and the union members. Such attempts at breaking some limitations adhering to professional work-styles, were also implied by the overall project design. All three projects were set up with a view to integrating the communication of results with the research process itself. This is most clearly reflected by the role of the working groups as well as by the design of the inquiries and debates. Besides, this also affected the attitudes to the publishing of results from the projects, where less attention were paid to reporting in the traditional scientific style.

The condition for the project work, it should not only result in reports in the traditional sense, was partly counteracted by the fact that the trade union projects were parts of the established research system with regard to the application for grants and accordingly, the reporting of results. This gave rise to a demand that the projects should be documented in the ordinary way. All the trade union projects thus resulted in a substantial production of reports, several volumes for each project. However, in many other respects the projects represented a departure from established patterns in the research system. This applies from the research user's point of view as well as from a professional point of view.

Opposed to dominant trends within research policies, the projects in many ways formed an alliance between researchers and users. The function of this alliance was to provide groups of potential research users, which traditionally had little direct contact with the research system, with opportunities to draw on research.

From a user's point of view, the projects could in other words be regarded as an attempt at opening channels to institutions which command knowledge resources that are potentially important to the users. This knowledge appeared particularly interesting and important because the trade unions, through the projects, saw an opportunity not only to learn, but also influence technical change processes which were expected to occur at the work-places.

From a researcher's point of view, the projects have been regarded as an opportunity to breaking established dividing-lines in the research system. Partly, such dividing-lines are associated with the various special fields (professions), and partly, with a fundamental division between the development and application of knowledge. The trade union projects made the point that development of knowledge was to take place in close connection with actual use of knowledge. This would also affect the professional orientation of the projects, which from the start were connected with a research institution with competence within computer science. The projects would at least imply a professional reorientation in these respects: on the one hand, purely technical criteria or criteria based on disciplines of computer science could not be used to decide upon the category of problems in the projects; furthermore, the question what was relevant knowledge for the projects, could not be decided by traditional divisions into subjects or professions.

The arguments for such professional reorientation, were primarily to be found in an interpretation of what were the interests of the trade union movement with regard to the need for knowledge about technical change processes. In all the projects one was concerned that the new technology to be used for planning and control purposes in the enterprises could lead to a monopoly of knowledge with the management. The trade union movement wanted to counteract this and consider the introduction of new technology in the light of its own objectives, primarily the objective of industrial democracy.

On the one hand, the demand for knowledge in the trade union movement was motivated by the *redistribution of knowledge* in line with the objective of democratization. On the other hand, *new knowledge* was needed about impacts of technical change and how objectives and interests of the trade union movement were affected. Besides, there were practical reasons for more knowledge, because the unions had to handle the various cases relating to technical change at the work-places.

Against this background, an approach built on traditional concepts of technology would be inadequate. This is partly because such concepts imply knowledge of technical solutions to problems 'by themselves', with no regard to the social implications of such solutions. Partly, traditional concepts of technology would be unsatisfactory because a certain monopoly of knowledge with the 'experts' is implied.

On such considerations, what could be termed a deprofessionalized concept of technology is justified. But this is no obvious tendency in the projects. There is also a tendency towards reprofessionalization, which concerns the need for knowledge about impacts of new technology. For instance, this could consist of a particular combination across disciplines, of knowledge of technical solutions – like data processing – and knowledge of various social aspects of technology. The latter type of knowledge would be related to a social science tradition.[†]

6.2 The trade union projects and related research

For some years, there has been an increasing interest in research on social impacts of EDP (or 'new technology'). Various subjects have been focused on, like conditions for and forms of employee participation, as well as codetermination by relevant interests and groups. This research trend would also include the trade union projects, thereby allowing the discussion on various aspects of the projects, like results, project design, working methods etc. compared to other research dealing with problems within the wider 'EDP and society' problem field.[‡] Among other things, such discussions could clarify the terms by which an evaluation of the trade union projects could be made.

During the project period, evaluations and positions were much affected by the various attitudes, political or professional, held towards the projects. The trade union projects thereby raised some controversy, because they were criticizing established professional positions as well as dominant trends within research policy.

On the one hand, the trade union projects have been considered a breakthrough for a new approach to the study of technical change processes. This is because the projects were incorporating a perspective of social interests by rejecting the 'neutral' and the 'objective', and by aiming at investigating the introduction of new technology at the work-places in the light of an underlying conflict of interests between the buyer and seller of labour.

Opinions of this kind illustrate that the evaluations of the projects have been marked by political fluctuations. The Iron and Metal Project, for example, coincided with an increasing criticism of established professional attitudes and research methods, at the end of the 1960s and the beginning of the 1970s.

[†] The social science tradition is not equally evident in all the trade union projects. The relationship with social science is particularly emphasized by the last project, the Chemical Industry Project, where a discussion on the project design and the results of the project, viewed in the light of related research traditions, is included.

[‡] The introduction to this book by Fjalestad discusses the status of the 'social impacts of EDP' research work.

Against this background, the project assumed an offensive character, an attempt at using research in order to influence the power relations at the work-places.[†]

On the other hand, the attempts at introducing a non-professional approach as well as the union policy orientation, have given rise to contentions that the trade union projects had little to do with research: apart from temporarily assisting the unions in question, they would not offer anything of value. Such criticism mostly stemmed from traditional technological disciplines and, perhaps, can be looked upon as an expression of opposition and uncertainty towards attempts at establishing new branches of knowledge.

To some extent, the kind of debate expressing positive or negative opinions, has been preventing a more fruitful discussion on the relationship between the trade union projects and other research. Still, the point has been made clearly that it is difficult to define the trade union projects in relation to traditional technological disciplines. Consequently, from these positions, fruitful discussion about research strategy becomes difficult.

Such discussions apparently are easier in relation to social science disciplines. For instance, there is a relationship at a fairly general level, concerning the project subjects as well as research methods. From their subject matter, the projects can be placed within a discipline which aims at investigating social aspects of technical change. Such studies have gained some ground in the social sciences, for example through investigations from the post-war period associated with the so-called 'automation debate', i.e. the study of social impacts of automation. This tradition became of current interest in the 1970s owing to the increasing use of EDP. In this field – in the new phase of the 'automation debate' – the trade union projects had some importance by taking up such questions at an early stage, at least in a Norwegian and Scandinavian perspective.

In the methodological sense, the projects offer many points of resemblance with action research. If by action research we mean an approach which is aiming at change and which is characterized by working methods implying that the researchers are to enter into a dialogue with, and act as partners in, the field which is to be changed, this description is valid for many of the trade union project activities. However, these projects differ from some action research by being characterized by attempts at clarifying problems and making project participants aware of the problems, rather than explicitly trying to solve them. In line with this, the trade union projects were putting problems under discussion, trying to encourage action rather, and were less directly involved in action (see especially the discussion on experiences from the Chemical Industry Project, section 4).

6.3 The trade union projects and Norwegian working life research
Within the social science tradition, the trade union projects could be included among a group of research, called working life research. On broad terms, this is

† This corresponds to some of the research policy slogans launched at that time: 'research for the trade union movement', 'research for the benefit of the wage-earners' etc.

characterized by a common problem field, but by a variety of particular problems studied, and by different approaches, methods etc. Within this many-sided field, there are some problems especially emphasized by the trade union projects, which also have been made current by the debate on social implications of new technology.

For one thing, there is the study of conditions for participation and of possibilities for developing a participative democratic system. The situation at the work-places has been regarded of great importance at this field. The possibilities for democratization have been associated with the design of jobs as well as the organization and promotion of the employees' interest. Norwegian working life research has been occupied with both these aspects.

The Industrial Democracy Project, run by the Work Research Institute in Oslo at the second half of the 1960s, focuses on the interaction of technical and social aspects of the work-place.[†] Underlying this project, it could be argued, there is an hypothesis that work-places which provide their occupants with opportunities for learning, better control of the overall working situation, good social contact etc. will in the long run give the employees the competence necessary to obtain greater influence on the overall economy. The trade union projects alternatively, are associating the possibilities for democratization with the organization of worker interests, taking as their starting points the existing union structure. An underlying hypothesis is that democratization will require a strengthening of the employees' interests, because the economy basically is characterized by unequal power relations.

The power structure will also influence the use of new technology. By the trade union projects, was assumed that EDP is constituting a field where the power to devise technical solutions and carry them into effect is particularly closely connected with knowledge of such solutions. Usually, EDP is introduced in such a way that the employees' experience and insight will not be utilized. Accordingly, the distribution of work-related knowledge will change, producing a weaker power position for the employees. By discussing these problems from a different point of view, compared to the working life research model represented by the Industrial Democracy Project and the so-called 'sociotechnical research', the trade union projects have provided important contributions to the further discussion on employee participation as well as codetermination during technical change (Fjalestad and Pape, 1979).

6.4 Implications for system development

The trade union projects have also been discussed in relation to another research field, made current by the introduction of new technology, i.e. strategies and

---

[†] Emery and Thorsrud (1969) and Gustavsen and Hunnius (1981) provide a discussion of the project ant its contexts. Gustavsen and Hunnius (1981) also discusses the experiences from the work organization experiments included in the project and its implications for working life reforms in Norway.

working methods for better system development. For one thing, such problems are connected with the general discussion on social implications of new technology. This is because the choice of approaches during system development probably could help avoiding unwanted effects of new systems. Neither is there any sharp division between the system development research field and the above-mentioned research field, i.e. the study of conditions for working life democracy. Probably, more democratic working methods during system development could affect the qualities of the working environment positively, thereby contributing to the democratization of the overall working life.

Against this background, the trade union projects have been considered an attempt at developing working methods for the introduction of new technology, in accordance with democratic requirements. The particular strategy emphasized by the projects is advocating close connections between the system development process and the organizing of employee interests by the unions. Among other things, this could imply a parallel development of working methods and regulation of interests by the negotiation and agreement system as well as by legislation.[†]

7 THE NORWEGIAN TRADE UNION MOVEMENT AND NEW TECHNOLOGY

At present, it is not easy to estimate the importance of the projects to the trade union movement. But although there are difficulties with pointing to particular effects, the projects can be placed in a context where they, in all appearances, have played a certain role.

During the trade union projects' period, there was a growing awareness among Norwegian trade unions of problems associated with the new, computer-based technology. These problems were expected to have a serious implications for the unions' interests. At the same time, related to this growing awareness of problems, the unions and the LO took measures to influence the processes of technical change in individual enterprises by means of specific 'data agreements'.[‡]

7.1 Trade union reform: data agreements

Negotiating separate agreements to emphasize and regulate particular fields of the many-sided relations between the parties is not an unusual phenomenon in Norwegian trade union tradition. Already in 1946, the associations in the private sector, LO and the Norwegian Employers' Confederation, negotiated a separate agreement on production committees in the companies. The purpose of this agreement was to further the cooperation between the local parties regarding the problems of production and higher productivity. (In 1966 this agreement

[†] Docherty (1980) discusses such problems in the light of Scandinavian experiences with trade union involvement in system development. Nygaard and Fjalestad (1981) present an account of relevant agreements and legislation as well as the implications for system development.

[‡] The origin of data agreements in Norway is briefly mentioned at the end of section 2. Below (section 7), this reform in trade union policy is discussed in more detail.

was converted to a general cooperation agreement and made a separate section of the Basic Agreement between LO and the Norwegian Employers' Confederation. See the specific section (1.2) on the Norwegian trade union movement included in this article.) The data agreements negotiated during the latter half of the 1970s add to the tradition of separate agreements. In particular, one could argue, the data agreements reinforce the tradition introduced by the original agreement on production committees. An important feature of this tradition is that problems concerning new technology in the individual enterprises are to be treated as matters of common interest to the local parties and accordingly, subject to local cooperation.

On the other hand, the data agreements also indicate a certain deviation from the tradition of cooperation dominating the field of technological development. This is due to the fact that these agreements are tying up the procedures for problem-solving and settling of disputes to the system of shop stewards and the regular trade union apparatus. In contrast, the agreement on production committees and the succeeding cooperation agreement recommend the use of separate cooperative bodies.

This change of strategy in union policy could be associated with a growing intention of taking stronger measures in order to control the use of technology. Probably, this is also indicating the seriousness of the problems experienced by the unions facing computer-based technologies. It looked as if those problems would create a situation where more efficient arrangements and channels of influence were needed than could be obtained by means of the coooperative bodies. Besides, the experiences with the works councils which had replaced the former production committees may also have been supporting the intention of bringing in the regular shop steward system. By and large, there had been difficulties in getting these committees active, and usually they were considered a less important part in the decision-making processes in the enterprises.

7.2 Union policies towards new technology

The introduction of data agreements could serve as a basis for a more thorough discussion of how union policies towards new technology are being formed. Obviously, trade unions' approach to matters of technology has various aspects and could not be treated satisfactorily by limiting the discussion to the negotiation of new agreements and the kind of provisions contained in these agreements.

The actual provisions of the data agreements suggest a certain difference between the general field of technology and the 'new technology', i.e. EDP. This difference has been an inherent property of trade union policies from the late 1960s when the Norwegian trade union movement became aware of the potential problems resulting from extensive use of EDP. Put another way, the data agreements present themselves as an important outcome of a process which finds its base in the recognition of EDP by members of the unions as 'problems'. This in turn, would release two kinds of discussions: what are the effects and problems arising from EDP and what measures could be taken to bring the use of EDP into accord with union goals?

The discussion of possible effects and problems has been going on during the 1970s. Various branches of the trade union movement have been involved thus, taking more sectors of the economy into consideration. Some of the LO unions have concluded their discussions by issuing separate policy statements with regard to EDP.

The discussion of possible measures for planning and control also tends to emphasize the special importance of EDP to the trade union movement. Besides negotiating formal agreements, there have been several attempts at carrying these agreements into effect. Mainly this has been done by establishing arrangements within the unions in order to identify and observe the special problem field as well as trying to build up the capacities that are required for handling these problems.

So, the process of policy formation has affected trade union organization. Besides, there are outcomes of this process with direct bearings on other 'actors' than the unions themselves. For instance, this is observed with regard to the practising of the procedures for planning and control specified by data agreements.

With regard to the first question raised, 'what are the problems?' the handling of problems of new technology by the trade union movement is related to how these problems are understood and, accordingly, to the interpretation of what are the actual interests of the unions and their members. For instance, according to the above-mentioned tradition of regarding new technology as a problem of higher productivity (cf. the production committees after the Second World War), the sharing of possible profits from installing a new system, production-line etc. would be focused on. This would also imply that the sharing of profits from higher productivity was to be effected by the stronger system, i.e. the negotiation of agreements by the shop stewards. Problems relating to system development work (ways and means of introducing new technology, working methods etc.) as well as the designing of new jobs were mainly considered matters of management interest, or were to be handled by cooperative bodies.

The data agreements imply a change of understanding of the problems of technical change by emphasizing the effects of new technology (in the first agreements the term 'computer-based system' was used) on employment, working environment etc. In other words, the question of *how* to use technology should become an important one, thus bringing a number of interests vital to the trade union movement into consideration.[†]

[†] Stressing the wider implications of technology, i.e. the new EDP-based technologies should not be considered in a purely 'technical' or economic perspective, the data agreements are contributing to a broader approach to the problems of working life. In this respect, the data agreements add to the Working Environment Act which has been influencing the attempts at working life reforms in Norway since the latter half of the 1970s. For a discussion of Norwegian working life reforms, see Gustavsen and Hunnius (1981).

With regard to the second question i.e. what measures could be taken, the handling of problems of technical change by the trade union movement is affected by the character of the mechanisms of problem-solving as well as conflict-resolution being applied. The data agreements are carrying on the tradition of common interests in matters of technology by emphasizing the importance of local cooperative arrangements. The agreements are also widening the field of such arrangements. According to the data agreements, cooperation should extend to the phases of planing and development of new systems as well as to implementation and evaluation. Cooperative arrangements should include employee representation by special shop stewards ('data shop stewards') as well as measures taken to carry out efficient training and proper information concerning new systems.

The links between the specific cooperative arrangements on the one hand and the regular shop steward system and union organization on the other make up an important feature of the data agreements. These links would imply a backing of the cooperative arrangements by an organizational element or mechanism of a different kind. Cooperation with regard to the utilization of EDP would not operate by itself but would be related to the very heart of the unions' manner of operation, i.e. the system of negotiations by shop stewards. Speaking in terms of systems or procedures and not of concrete cases, the data agreements therefore are opposing the idea of common interests in matters of technology by also linking these matters to a system which could operate on the basis of conflictual relations. Besides, the system of negotiation allows the unions to apply stronger means than are available within the field of cooperative arrangements.

The relationship between the different systems is demonstrated by the double position of the data shop steward. On the one hand, the data shop steward should act as a special representative by taking part in local cooperative arrangements. On the other hand according to the relations between the basic agreements and the data agreements (see the separate section (1.2) on the Norwegian trade union movement), the data shop steward should form a part of the regular shop steward system. In order to prevent split loyalties resulting from this double position, guidelines for the practising of data agreements issued by the LO recommend the data shop steward should join local union bodies.

Before discussing possible effects of the trade union projects, the process of policy formation and of designing formal instruments for the purpose of controlling the actual implications of EDP (in one word 'politicization' of the technology) could be summarized in the following five points.

(1) Knowledge formation
Assuming actual policies are relying on an understanding of the current problems, trade union policies towards EDP imply on the one hand, the application of a set of concepts and on the other hand, the building of experience. During this process, certain concepts would be considered appropriate by active union

members and consequently, would affect discussions within union bodies. These concepts in turn, are supporting the accumulation of knowledge as well as the expression of opinions by serving as a basis for the interpretation of experience and allowing the mediation of these experiences within the trade union movement.

The relationship between the underlying concepts and the building of experiences probably would have a more complex character than is suggested by the rather general discussion above. Besides, to collect the materials necessary to allow an account of the actual development of trade union opinions with regard to EDP presents a research task of its own. Still, there are some obvious trends within the overall picture to suggest a change in opinions. An important aspect of this change is made up by the substitution of a rather narrow perspective oriented at the 'technical' prospects of the new technology, by a broader more socially oriented perspective. The concepts which have been applied to express the implications of technology cover the topics of control of technology by society, impacts on working environment, codetermination by employees, impacts on employment, efficient organization of production etc.

Taking these new attitudes into consideration, still there is the question to what extent they have been built on the experiences actually undergone by trade union members, or to what extent they are reflecting generally changing attitudes towards working life problems also influencing the opinions of the trade union movement.[†] In either case, the change of attitudes and of opinions presents evidence to the politicization of problems of technology.

At the start, the process of knowledge formation on the topic 'EDP' within the trade union movement probably would be hard to distinguish from the understanding of the same topic arising in the society in general. Concerning the needs for acquiring new knowledge, the situation in the unions as well as in other parts of society was marked by a widely felt uncertainty on the possible effects of the new technology. Most trade union members had little or no experience at all with the use of EDP at their work-places and consequently, tended to consider it an expert matter. Gradually, at first limited to only a few industries, there was an increased understanding of the impacts of the various applications of EDP on the shop floor.

(2) Interest orientation

Confronted with a situation marked by uncertainty both with regard to the actual directions of the technological development and, to the wider implications, the trade union movement reacted by demanding control of the technology by society. Generally, this demand would imply an attempt at interpreting trade union interests into an established political context and also trying to solve the 'new' problems by means of 'old' policies. The effect of the new technology on

† See the footnote concerning the Working Environment Act on p. 57.

trade union interest orientation thereby would be to emphasize a set of goals of which the unions already were approving.

At the shop level, the demand for control by society is closely related to the demand for codetermination by elected employee representatives (see the arrangements for industrial democracy discussed in the section (1.2) on the Norwegian trade union movement). In this respect, it could be argued, the new technology has been contributing to a deeper understanding of the implications of codetermination in the technological field. For instance, this is expressed by the demand that the systems for planning and control being applied by the individual firms should be subject to union influence.

On the other hand, the growing awareness of the impacts of new technology apparently has released trade union discussion on problems of a new kind. More precisely, there is a group of problems now being emphasized, which according to traditional interest orientation, for the most part were not recognized. This includes: the problems of work organization; the need for jobs that allow more fully the utilization of workers' abilities and the building up of knowledge resources; the need for local control systems that allow employee participation; the demand for union control at all levels concerning the utilization of new technology; etc.[†]

(3) Organizational development

The third aspect of the politicization of EDP by the trade union movement could be described as attempts at internal organizational development. Within this general trend there are various types of measures taken in order to build up organizational resources.

Firstly, there are attempts at defining new tasks related to the specific problems presented by the technology. Because of the character of these problems, as well as the increasing impact of EDP, the unions were confronted with certain dilemmas. On the one hand, there is the problem of giving priorities to the various tasks, or simply finding a place for new activities within organizations already experiencing a strain on capacities. On the other hand, the problem is not only of a quantitative nature: there is also the problem of adapting the unions' working modes. For instance, a dominant aspect of technological problems concerns the long-range building of knowledge which, typically, would be difficult to handle for organizations like the unions that are mostly oriented towards day-to-day problem-solving activities.[‡]

[†] The issues raised by the trade union movement also justify, to some extent, emphasizing the differences between trade union interest orientation and the public debate concerning the social implications of EDP. In Norway, public debate has been focussing on the protection of personal integrity with regard to computer-based personal registers (see the legislation on this matter, footnote p. 57. Recently, there has also been an extensive debate on possible employment effects of new technology. These issues have also been raised by the trade unions but are regarded as parts of the overall interest orientation.

[‡] See the discussion on working modes in the special section (1.2) on the Norwegian trade union movement.

Next, there is the introduction of new organizational forms as well as procedures for dealing with 'data problems' within unions at local and central levels. Examples of these arrangements are the 'data shop steward', the 'data committees', the special programmes for educating shop stewards and ordinary union members in 'data problems', etc. For instance, within most branches of the Norwegian trade union movement many local unions and works clubs today are naming data shop stewards as a matter of routine.

During the last five years, the special programmes for education in data problems and the training of data shop stewards have been becoming a separate part of overall Norwegian trade union education. Some of these programmes are operated from the central level (by LO and the special Workers' Educational Association as well as by some national unions). In addition, there are programmes and special courses run by local unions.

There are then attempts at adapting union management to new tasks, activities, programmes, etc. Generally, this problem has been raised with regard to communication as well as cooperation within the overall shop steward apparatus. As one type of solution, some unions and works clubs have included the data shop stewards in their regular managing bodies.

(4) Instruments for planning and control

The fourth aspect of the politicization of EDP concerns the forming of specific instruments for the regulations of EDP applications. In principle, there are two types of formal instruments: agreements concerning the relations between negotiating parties and legislation stating general goals and procedures for the utilization of this technology.[†] From the trade union point of view, both are usually considered instruments for planning and control, i.e. instruments constituting the basis for potential local action to influence concrete EDP applications.[‡]

(5) Institutionalization

At a general societal level, legislation as well as agreements are contributing to the institutionalization of the EDP field. This implies the association of interests

[†] The first General Agreements on Computer-based Systems were concluded in 1975, firstly between the LO and the Norwegian Employers' Confederation and then between the state and the various associations of civil servants. In 1978, the local government sector got a corresponding Agreement. The General Agreements on Computer-based Systems have later been revised in connection with the revisions of the Basic Agreements of the different sectors. (See the discussion on Basic Agreements in the section (1.2) on the Norwegian trade union movement).

The Act relating to Workers' Protection and Working Environment (usually referred to as the Working Environment Act) came into force in 1977. Section 12, which deals with the arrangement of work in general and also has a separate heading for planning and control systems, particularly applies to the utilization of new technology.

Another law that also applies to EDP is the Act on Personal Registers which came into force in 1980.

[‡] See the discussions on trade union policies in the section (1.2) on the trade union movement in Norway.

with goals, procedures and rules for the application of this particular technology. The implementation of these rules etc. is left to the parties of the labour market and to specific state agencies. (See the combination of collective agreements and state regulation in the Norwegian industrial relations' system, section 1.2).

7.3 The effects of the trade union projects

In relation to union policies, the trade union projects probably had influence on several levels.

First, there is the question of building knowledge on the actual use of EDP. The projects investigated the relations between technical solutions, the applications of such solutions and, the properties of work and working environment. However, it is not easy to estimate how much knowledge, in the strict sense of the world — empirical and systematically collected knowledge — the projects have furnished. There are difficulties with 'measuring' the creation of knowledge in the respective unions. Besides, the purpose of the projects was not to provide knowledge as such, though the creation of knowledge has been considered an important element. It is also essential to make clear which questions should be studied, thereby making up the overall approach to the problems. So, instead of discussing the question of knowledge 'as such', it is probably more fruitful to regard to the construction of the unions' approach to problems of technology. In this respect, there is a striking correspondence between the themes of the projects and the topics which recently have been affecting trade union discussions on new technology. These are mainly the topics of planning and control, workplace experiences as well as possibilities for learning, and trade union organization with regard to the effecting of influence and the accumulation of knowledge. Although it cannot be claimed the projects have caused such discussions, the various project activities have apparently contributed to the forming of the approaches taken by the unions. Regarding the various aspects of the unions' politicization of the new technology, there seems to be a relationship between the trade union projects and the processes of knowledge formation as well as interest orientation. But certainly, it is difficult to estimate in what ways the projects have had an effect, considering other factors which possibly also have been influencing the understanding of EDP in the trade union movement.

Besides the building of knowledge and understanding of trade union interests, the projects were to approach the problem of how to connect such processes with union work. The experiences with the particular methods introduced by the local working groups provide some insight into this problem. During project work, these groups were functioning more or less the way they were planned. (There were variations between the projects and difficulties which had to be solved in various ways, so the actual course of local group work to some extent shifted from one project to another.) On the other hand, there is the experience that local group work had to rely on support from the central level as well as the problems and difficulties met with regard to the spreading of group activities.

This seems to raise a number of problems. First, the spreading of group activities apparently will require a certain input of resources from the central level and accordingly, there is the problem of how this could be effected by the central union bodies: what kind of support is required, how could the various supportive activities be organized, etc.?

Besides, there is also the problem of how and to what extent this particular element of union work could be adopted, in relation to the prevailing short-range, problem-solving activities of the union bodies. The problem of getting the local groups work in with day-to-day union activities was made apparent during the projects and became particularly evident when project work was finished.

Although, the trade union projects did not solve any of these problems, the problems were raised by the projects and, the context within which they had to be solved was to some extent made clear by the project work. The trade union projects pointed to the need for establishing close relations between the unions' work with EDP-problems and prevailing themes as well as activities within the overall union work. This could be done, and it was accentuated by the projects, by relating the 'EDP-work' to the ordinary shop stewards' work for instance, by means of the particular 'data shop steward' arrangement. Another way of linking EDP to prevailing union activities, which actually was explored by the projects, is the incorporation of EDP as a subject by the educational programme of the trade union movement.[†]

Another important effort of the projects, which perhaps is easier to point out, is the contribution of the project activity to the development of instruments for control as well as related organizational measures taken by the trade union movement. The central example is the idea of separate data agreements. This was first discussed during the first project, Iron and Metal. However, a local data agreement was first introduced at Viking/Askim, a company producing tyres for cars, bicycles etc. which comes within the organization of the Chemical Workers' Union. Shortly after the Viking/Askim agreement had been concluded, the General Agreement between the LO and the Norwegian Employers' Confederation was established. This agreement was founded on the first local agreement and was generalizing the principles stated. Furthermore, the General Agreement opened the way for new agreements, both local agreements and agreements comprising whole industries. The General Agreement has also influenced certain provisions in the Working Environment Act, particularly as regards employee participation during the introduction of systems for planning and control.

The example of data agreements and the rights and possibilities these agreements give to the trade union movement regarding participation, codetermination,

---

[†]The concept 'data shop steward' appeared during the Iron and Metal Project. With regard to educational activities, the forming of programmes, courses etc. was a central element of all the projects. Some of the EDP-related themes, subjects, and materials worked out by the projects have later been used by the LO as well as by the unions in their regular courses.

training etc., shows a direct connection between ideas and experimental activities in the trade union projects and the development of union policies towards data technology. Therefore, it could be claimed, by introducing patterns of action which could be carried on by the unions, the projects have influenced the politicization of EDP. Such effects can to some extent be explained by the working methods in the projects and particularly the close ties with the trade union organization, on the local as well as the central level. The projects were partly mixed with ordinary organization work, and in some respects acted as a kind of supplement to the regular organization.

One effect of this, apart from a temporary supply of extra resources in the unions, is that the project work in a way has provided solutions to the problem 'EDP' for the trade union movement. These are solutions in the form of some measures and working methods that can be introduced by central and local bodies. The closeness to the organization has ensured that models worked out in the projects were in line with established patterns of action in the unions.

Besides the action models or the proposals concerning which measures could be taken, there is the question to what extent the trade union projects have resulted in action. (See the central project purpose quoted from the Iron and Metal Project.) In the local unions involved, there was a flourishing of activities during project work, and to some extent after the projects were finished. But it was made clear, particularly the working group method was less suitable for spreading to other unions or to other fields of union activity than those defined by the projects. Accordingly, what was considered a radical reform of union work did not have the response which might have been expected.

There is also the question of the relationship between the trade union projects and the overall level of activity among union members with regard to EDP problems. To expect an increasing level of activity to result from the projects obviously is very ambitious, and the projects hardly had such effects. Besides, increased activity throughout the trade union movement will probably not occur as a result from research projects, but will have to be effected by regular processes of union work.

8 CONCLUSION

One of the central subjects in the Norwegian debate on EDP problems has been the question of planning and control of technology. In this debate the trade union movement has played an active part and contributed to the designing of control measures like the General Agreements and the Working Environment Act. Closely related to the development of such control measures, attitudes to, as well as an understanding of, EDP problems have been adopted by the trade union movement, which claim EDP should be used in accordance with central political objectives such as democratic control of the economy and good working environment. The trade union movement has also taken steps within its own organization in the form of general arrangements and models for the handling of technical change within enterprises.

At present it seems reasonable to view the role of the trade union projects in the light of such braod change processes. Rather than look for particular results or effects, it will be more fruitful to consider the projects as parts of a development which from the trade union movement's point of view has many interesting aspects. The primary ones probably are the designing of control measures towards the new technology and the parallel development of understanding and knowledge as well as the adaptation of union working methods. But also the aspects of the projects relating to research and research policy have apparently had some importance beyond the project work. The projects have demonstrated an approach to technical change processes which allow the formulation of problems and research purposes on the basis of conflicts of interests. The projects also form examples of a research strategy implying the cooperation of the employee side of the enterprises and research institutions. By the very fact that the project work has comprised a rather large spectrum of the trade union movement and was, more or less, carried on for a decade, it probably has provided good opportunities for obtaining insight into the possibilities and problems attached to this research model.

Planning and control have an organizational aspect, i.e. the patterns of organizational handling of the problems by participants and parties in the decision-making processes. The subject also involve a varying degree of participation from union members as well as actions at local and central levels. In the trade union projects this subject has been formulated as a question of how to effect local action supported by activities at the central level. The projects have not given any final answers to this question which still makes up an urgent matter for the trade union movement. This is related to a dilemma concerning the unions capacities for influencing the use of new technology. On the one hand, there is the set of rights and opportunities with regard to system development work and the decision-making processes. On the other hand, there are accumulated experiences pointing to the lack of actual use of such rights and opportunities by the unions. The different agreements negotiated by the unions and the amendments to these agreements, do not solve the problem of how the individual union could make its influence more effective.

REFERENCES

Docherty, Peter (1980) User participation in and influence on systems design, in Bjørn-Andersen (ed.), *The Human Side of Information Processing*, papers from the Copenhagen Conference on Computer Impact 1978, Amsterdam, North-Holland.

Emery, F. E., and Thorsrud, E. (1969) *Form and Content in Industrial Democracy*, London, Tavistock.

Fjalestad, J., and Pape, A. (1979) Research on social aspects of computerization and democratization of working life, in Samet (ed.), *Papers from Euro IFIP 1979*, Amsterdam, North-Holland/IFIP.

Gustavsen, B., and Hunnius, G. (1981) *New Patterns of Work Reform. The Case of Norway*, Oslo, Universitetsforlaget.

Norwegian Federation of Trade Unions (1978), International Office, Norwegian Federation of Trade Unions, Oslo.

Nygaard, K. (1977) The Iron and Metal Project. Trade union participation, *Proceedings of CREST Conference on Management Information Systems 1977*, London, Cambridge University Press.

Nygaard, K., and Bergo, O. T. (1975) The trade unions. New users of research, *Personnel Review*, **4**, 2.

Nygaard, K., and Fjalestad, J. (1981) Group interests and participation in information system development, *Microelectronics, Productivity and Employment*, OECD, Paris.

Sandberg, Å. (ed.) (1979) *Computers Dividing Man and Work*, Stockholm, Arbetslivscentrum.

Technology and employment

Arne Maus

1 INTRODUCTION

The question of whether EDP has an impact on employment, is one of the most controversial issues concerning the social impact of technology. Some people claim that we are facing increasing unemployment, caused to a large degree by automation, in which EDP is an increasingly important element. In Europe, unemployment is now increasing annually. In highly industrialized countries like Belgium and Great Britain, the unemployment rate amounted to approximately 10 per cent of the labour force at the turn of the year 1980/81.

This is nonsense, other people maintain. Viewed over a longer term technological progress has not created unemployment. Admittedly, there are problems when fewer employees are required in some jobs, and must seek employment elsewhere. However, the automation process itself and the growth resulting from an increase in productivity will in a few years' time give employment to more people, not fewer. *But as figures show*

Historical facts seem to support the latter opinion, whereas a reference to the last five or seven years could support the more pessimistic argument.

There are also those who deny the relevance of the question itself. Such a complex debate cannot be discussed within the limited scope of technology. Only a total framework embracing, for example, socio-political factors could give a satisfactory answer. This is a theoretical point of departure, which at its most extreme implies that a discussion of technology becomes meaningless. We dissociate ourselves from this view. A technological approach as well as a more general analysis seems to be required. This article could to a large extent be regarded as a data-technological approach to the question.

As a starting point, we wish to presuppose that the choice of technology (machines and knowledge of their application) is itself significant, and to a large extent influences the way production is organised, and, the output of goods and services. Existing technology determines the framework of the organization of production. Changes in technology, could imply new bases for organizing production because various cost factors are altered and new production methods and products become possible. Without technological progress there will be no further automation. The realistic alternatives given by an existing technology, will therefore set the limit to discussion of the impact of this technology.

This concept forms the bases of our discussion. Our approach is to divide the article into three sections. The first section discusses EDP technology and its characteristic features from an employment perspective. Secondly we will describe experience gained up to the present as regards how EDP and related technologies can influence a number of jobs. (A common term for these is 'new technology', which comprises communications technology and industrial automation technology — sensors and servo mechanisms — in addition to EDP). A part of this description is a summary of results from a recent investigation on the impact of EDP on employment in the office. Finally the perspective will be widened to the total labour market, employment trends and unemployment examined from a more general viewpoint, with an attempt to draw conclusions from the points discussed.

2 CHARACTERISTICS OF EDP TECHNOLOGY

2.1 What is EDP?

Computers and similar electronic devices, consist of an interconnection of one or more micro-electronic circuits (also termed integrated circuits). These micro-electronic circuits are small, square chips made of a glassy material (silicon). The size including plastic mounting is approximately 1 X 3 cm. From 1000 to more than 200 000 transistors and semiconductors have been etched into the surface of the chip by means of a photolithographic technique to make a fine-meshed network. Every year, the number of transistors possible to etch into such a chip is nearly doubled.

In order to understand the costs of various applications of micro-technology it is important to distinguish between several levels at which the technology can be employed.

(1) Integrated circuits (chips)

The type of integrated circuits required have to be mass-produced, so that they can be sold and development costs written off in the course of a few years. The market penetration price of a chip may be high, but after a year of mass production the price will normally fall to between $10 and $1 each. Products at this level are integrated circuits like microprocessors or the circuitry of a pocket calculator.

(2) Construction, physical surroundings

Usually several integrated circuits have to be connected to convey meaningfull messages to the surrounding. In additon to making a connection diagram, one has to place the components on circuit boards, ensure power supply, housings etc. This complex electronic unit is connected to the outside world through a screen, a keyboard, and interfaces. Products at this level are general computers, quartz watches or industrial robots.

(3) Programming

Electronic units produced in larger series are normally general, i.e. they can potentially perform a lot of functions. A unit is given a particular function when it is programmed for this particular function – i.e. when rules for the function are incorporated in the electronics. Products of this kind are a computer which is in charge of an invoice system or an electronic cash register which is given particular functions.

(4) As part of a larger technical system

A programmed electronic unit, either in the form of a computer, industrial robot or a telephone exhange, normally has to be connected with other machines or data processing components to function in a meaningful way. There are examples like an industrial robot connected with an assembly line or a telephone exchange connected with the telephone network.

(5) As part of an organization

A data processing system or an automated machine system with 'incorporated' electronics has to be accepted in an organization (a firm, a public body, the home) to be of use. The problems in accomplishing this are often underestimated or totally disregarded. It is parts of this level this book deals with.

Very roughly we can say that every level of this chain increases the costs of production 5 to 10-fold. A certain amount of electronics can therefore be mass-produced for watches, cars or TV sets (level 2 or 3) at a fraction of what it costs to introduce the same amount of electronics as a general computer system in an organization (level 5). There is also a time lag at each of these levels. Today's use is based on integrated circuits that were introduced approximately 4–5 years ago.

Moreover, on each of these levels there are certain general conditions (social, financial, access to qualified labour etc.) that influence the choice made on the level in question. This sets obvious limitations as to what type of technology will eventually be applied.

To sum up, we can say that financial aspects of EDP technology favour:

– mass production and standard designs;
– direct integration of control electronics into various products.

The costs of the chips only, can almost always be overlooked when discussing the introduction of technology in an organization. The dominating costs of

the machines could amount to 50 per cent of total costs only in very large services like the postal servies, banks, tax offices etc., where one design can be
duplicated in thousands, or for example a small enterprise which purchases the
same standard system as thousands of other enterprises (for example salaries
and wages, accounting, text processing).

2.2 Why is EDP technology important now?

EDP technology will constantly be employed for new purposes, and the total
data processing power available for various purposes will increase considerably
in the course of the 1980s. There are three principal reasons behind this.

(1) EDP is a general tool

Data processing technology is applicable to a series of different tasks. The tasks
to be transferred to EDP have the common features that they are often repetitive
or highly structured (or both). Only where there are poorly structured, non-
repetitive tasks, has automation been ignored.

(2) Prices are constantly falling

It has been a recent trend that the cost of a particular micro-electronic circuit
falls by 50 per cent per year, whereas the cost of a particular computer goes
down by 25 per cent per year. (Noyce, 1977). Technological and other factors,
like financial resources required etc., indicate that this trend will not diminish
in the 1980s. It is therefore not unlikely that the coming ten years will show an
equally high growth rate as today.

(3) Micro-electronics are small

EDP being generally applicable and inexpensive is not sufficient. It is also an
essential factor that the technology is now so small and nearly maintenance-free
that it can be installed in all possible types of equipment and machines. The
diminishing size for a particular function, makes micro-electronics increasingly
usable.

Already today, you can have a complete computer on a single micro-
electronic chip. By 1985, it will be possible to place what corresponds to today's
large computers on such a chip. Therefore in a few years time, there will be few
finanicial or functional limitations to the processing power that can be incorporated into a product.

To illustrate the immense increase in the use of micro-electronics to date we will
take a look at Table 1 showing, among other things, the number of computers
in use. Please note that this table only shows the number of computers. It has
to be added that each machine in a given year is considerably faster and has
a much larger storage capacity (memory) than a computer five or ten years
earlier.

Table 1

Geographical distribution of computers in numbers and the total value of installed data processing equipment in thousand million dollars

	1960		1970		1978	
	number	value	number	value	number	value
USA	5 500	8.8	65 000	92.6	200 000	193.6
Western Europe	1 500	2.6	21 000	40.5	110 000	124.8
Japan	400	0.5	6 000	7.5	45 000	49.6
Others	1 600	0.8	18 000	9.6	95 000	72.0
Sum total	9 000	12.7	110 000	150.2	450 000	424.0

(Source: Diebold Europe, 1979, according to Rada, 1980.)

When considering the number of computers and the processing capacity of each machine in the respective years, it is easy to estimate that, provided these tendencies in the use of EDP continue in the 1980s, the data processing capacity in use around 1990 will be between 20 and 100 times the size of the data processing capacity in use today. (The estimate varies according to how 'processing capacity' is defined.)

Given the present level of use of EDP, the relative balance of power between groups and classes in society in the 1980s could obviously be greatly disturbed. Considerable changes in the way of organizing economic life and society as a whole may occur. We will let most of these problems lie, some are mentioned in other articles in this book. Even so, it is important to stress that one must not be blinded by figures. Even though, for example, one computer in 1980 made a certain number of employees redundant, it is by no means certain that in 1985, two computers will make twice as many employees redundant. Applications, prices, attitudes and the possibilities of controlling technology change continuously. It is, however, not unlikely that such a heavy increase in the use of EDP which is expected in the 1980s, will accentuate existing features of the development up to now.

It is also possible that completely new impacts will be observed due to a marked increase in the use of technology — elements which today seem unimportant or do not exist. For example, in the 1960s it would seem rather odd to ponder on what impact it would have if every home had access to more processing power than the contents of an average computer. In the 1980s this is obviously a relevant question. However, we do not want to include such 'outlandish' impacts, but rather to discuss a possible accentuation of existing prominent features.

2.3 EDP and unemployment

In the discussion as to whether technology could create long-lasting unemployment, the central question is whether EDP represents something new in technical progress. Some people talk about a new industrial revolution. Other people maintain that this is a steady continuation of the technical progress that has taken place over the last one to two hundred years. If the latter opinion holds true, it would, as mentioned in the introduction, be right to point out that the enormous technical progress we have seen up to now has not created long-lasting unemployment. We should not be too worried about tendencies within EDP — the problems occuring will at most be transitionary.

However, several factors indicate that the development within EDP foreshadows something new as compared with previous mechanization and technical progress. We cannot take the easy way out and apply experience from the relation between mechanization and technical progress during the last two hundred years to what is happening now. The following points support this view:

(1) A lot more tasks can be automated with EDP than could be mechanized in the past

Up to the present, automation and mechanization have largely shown two main characteristics. One has been to divide existing tasks into several more specialized operation. At the same time, control of the work has often been separated from the performance itself. In every such (more or less) specialized operation, one has attempted to replace muscular strength by machines — either by introducing machines in manual work or by replacing outdated machines by new and more labour-saving machines. While formerly machines were installed to do the manual operations, EDP technology can now be used to automate *both* functions, i.e. the specialized operations as well as control of the work.

The following are examples of EDP replacing mechanics: the insides of telephone exchanges, telex appratus and watches can now be entirely composed of data technology. Examples where EDP takes over control/planning of the work ('brainwork') are: assessment of pension and taxes in the public sector, the control of a welding robot at an assembly line, planning of the production in a larger enterprise, the performance of complicated engineering calculations or the moving and adjustment of texts in text processing equipment. Consequently, EDP has drastically increased the number of operations it is possible to automate.

EDP will enter 'all' occupational groups and lines of business, and therefore it cannot be taken for granted that redundant manpower from one sector (plus young people seeking their first job) can be employed in another sector with increasing demand for personnel. Those who formerly were made redundant because of rationalization in agriculture, mainly went into the manufacturing industries. The growth in employment over the past few years has almost exclusively taken place in private and public services. Also these area of the economic life, which earlier were protected from automation, will be subject to automation in the 1980s.

(2) EDP automation proceeds faster than previous mechanization and the speed of introduction strongly increases

Up to now, the speed of introduction has at least doubled every second year. If this increase is going to continue, and there are few indications to the contrary, EDP will in the 1980s be used to such an extent in trade and industry that no-one should be surprised if it results in far more negative impacts on empolyment than occur today, even though each application could have a limited effect.

(3) The ratio of price to output of data components and computers has declined by 25–30 per cent in annual average over the last 20 years

This fall in prices seems to increase at the threshold of the 1980s. In previous mechanization there has been no correspondingly strong and long-lasting fall in prices on such significant factors. In other words: where it at present is technically feasible to utilize automated equipment, these solutions will also 'soon' become cheaper than employees who now are performing this work. Thereby EDP will become increasingly competitive with human labour. On the other hand, there is the factor, as mentioned earlier, that expenses for the machines only constitute a part of the total costs. It is, however, likely that also total costs of the use of EDP will generally show a relative decrease compared with labour costs. When an automated service becomes considerably cheaper than a manual one, it does not have to be identical to be preferred to a more labour demanding service, for example, washing machines, hoovers, etc. instead of domestic servants, ticket-issuing machines on buses and the underground instead of conductors, bank machines instead of employees, etc. (J. Gershuny, 1978).

(4) The computer industry and applications of EDP employ relatively few people

In Norway in 1980 appoximately 25 000 employees, or a little less than 1.5 per cent of the total workforce was employed in this area. The EDP sector alone cannot absorb any large number of jobless people.

(5) The reliability of EDP technology is very high

The point is not that EDP systems always provide 'correct' answers. We have all experienced or heard about EDP systems making great blunders. But the important thing is that when a data processing system is put into operation, it will not be exposed to wear in the ordinary sense — it operates the way it should year after year, almost maintence-free. Where EDP is used to replace mechanics or electromechanics, the need for repair and maintenance will drop drastically.

(6) The growth in data technology is only comparable with radical changes like the introduction of electricity

But as opposed to electricity, data technology has, up to now not created a demand for new large groups of products or a new infrastructure in society. The large growth expected from data technology is the use of old and new services from the State Telecommunication Administration (data network, viewdata, telefax etc.). The State Telecommunication Administration (PTT) in Norway has recently presented a long-term project lasting until 1993, proposing a large-scale investment programme of £4.25 milliard to increase the capacity considerably and offer new services by means of new technology (NOU 10, 1981). The net demand is approximately 2200 new employees during that period, or a price per new job of nearly £2 million. The companies that are going to supply the bulk of the new equipment which the State Telecommunication Administration is going to install, Standard Telefon og Kabelfabrik and Elektrisk Bureau, expect a slow decline in the number of employees in the years to come. I do not think it is much of an exaggeration to say that an investment of £4.25 milliard over a period of 12 years will hardly create a single new job in Norway as a whole. This is not only a good and important example of increase in activity by means of EDP. The undertaking is also so large in itself that it will tie up a considerable proportion of the funds that annually are intended for investments in Norway, and which otherwise could be used to create new jobs.

As a summing-up, we can say that the six above-mentioned points *do not* prove that EDP necessarily will lead to extensive or long-lasting unemployment. There are, however, distinctive features of EDP which makes it potentially more problematic, compared with previous technical progress, when it comes to keeping a low unemployment rate. Certainly, the present situation is different from previously, because the number of employees in the manufacturing industries is declining, whereas before 1960 the number increased during the technical progress. Therefore, the question now seems to be whether the service industry can employ progressively more people despite a more widespread introduction of EDP, and not whether jobs are created in the manufacturing industries.

The weightiest argument to be made against the reasoning in the six points above, is in my opinion that provided all this correct, there will be a tremendous increase in productivity (i.e. production output per employee). This has not been the case over the past few years, it is the opposite if anything. The growth in productivity in the Western world has slowed down and nearly stagnated since 1973–75. One is tempted to wonder whether EDP has fooled people to believe in unrealistic prospects.

A reply to this objection would be that it is wrong to relate total productivity in society to the impacts of EDP, which is only one of the factors influencing productivity. EDP is not yet so widespread that productivity in EDP necessarily dominates the total productivity. In addition to EDP not being any essential factor in a total perspective, it is also generally believed that the profitability of EDP systems is increasing. As an example we can mention that Standard Telefon og Kabelfabrik has calculated an internal rate of return on their investments in EDP of 20 per cent for the period 1968–75, 50 per cent for 1976–80 and expects 70 per cent for planned projects for the years 1980—84 (Espeli and Maus, 1981b).

None the less, the low productivity theory is to some extent relevant. With a more widespreas use of EDP and the increase in productivity which, according to this article, will occur, EDP is in the course of the 1980s bound to contribute considerably to the total productivity in society. If this increase takes place, the two extreme ways in which it would occur are either that progressively fewer employees produce about the same quantities of goods and services (increasing unemployment), or that an increasing number of employees produce far more goods and services (like the period of growth enjoyed in the 1960s).

3 EXPERIENCE WITH EDP AND EMPLOYMENT

3.1 Individual examples

The previous reflections have mainly been general and 'theoretical'. There is, however, a series of individual examples of rationalization by means of EDP. The purpose of presenting these is partly to show the varied uses of EDP, and partly to document that EDP in some particular occupations or lines of business could contribute to a reduced demand for labour and/or a much improved productivity. But it must be underlined that these examples do not predict possible *total* impacts of EDP on employment.

The examples can be divided into two categories: conventional data processing — i.e. the application of general, normally large, computers, and examples where micro-electronics have been built into various products. (The examples from West Germany are collected from *Der Spiegel*, no. 16, 1978).

(1) Conventional data processing, the application of general computers
(a) Public administration
Central registers of real estate in Bayern, Hessen and Reinland-Pfalz — a change-over from manual systems to EDP technology resulted in a reduction of 4000 employees.

(b) Banking and insurance
In Norway there has been an actual increase of 42 per cent in total assets in banking for the period 1970—78. When measuring the quantity of work in banking in other ways, like the number of cashed cheques and bank giro transfers, it has increased at least fivefold. The number of employees has in the period 1971—78 increased by nearly 30 per cent. In insurance, employment has stagnated in the 1970s, and Norway's largest life insurance company has had a decline in the number of employees, from 415 in 1973 to 300 in 1979, despite a satisfactory increase in turnover. This can to a large degree be ascribed to the use of computer-based management information systems (Halvorsen, 1980).

Banking in West Germany: from 1962 to 1977, the trunover increased fivefold and the number of employees doubled. From 1973 to 1977 there was no increase in the number of employees.

(c) Health and social services

The social security information system in Norway will require £18 million and axe 255 positions at the six largest social security offices in the first phase. In the long term, one estimates a reduction of 1400 positions – i.e. 31 per cent of the employees in 1977. The employees have opposed these plans through their trade union, and it is hardly likely that the project will result in as high a reduction as 31 per cent. Since these plans were launched, the number of employees has not been increased, and in 1981 there has been a net reduction of a few positions. At the same time the social security offices have, since 1977, been loaded with more tasks (the new sickness benefit arrangement, the register of employers and employees).

(d) Wholesale and retail trade

The four largest chain store companies in West Germany have had a substantial increase in turnover and have reduced the number of employees by 3600 since 1973. This can largely be ascribed to rationalization based on EDP, particularly as regards *storage functions*.

(2) Data technology as integrated into another product, or applied as part of a production process

(a) Office automation

Text processing systems ('computer in the typewritter'): Halifax Building Society in England changed from automatic typewritters to text processing machines (16) and has trebled the output in the clerical department with the same manning (CIS, 1979). At a clerical department at Borregaard factories, manning was reduced from 14 to two employees by extensive use of standardized letters along with the introduction of text processing. IBM in Great Britain found that a change-over to text processing equipment among their 500 typists increased productivity by 148 per cent (*The Financial Times,* 3 April 1978). Reported increase in productivity is normally around 100 per cent, but the figures vary considerably. For other office automation, see the section of the chapter which sums up the results from the project 'EDP and employment in the office sector' in Espeli and Maus (1981a).

(b) Printing and allied industries in West Germany

80 000 fewer jobs in the course of two years (photocomposition and text processing).

   Since 1974, 600 jobs in the newspaper industry have been lost in Norway for the same reason. One example from the USA shows that when journalists can write their own material direct on screens connected with photocomposition machine the number of employees in the composing room can be reduced by 80 per cent over a few years (*The New Scientist* 30 November 78). These days one is negotiating about the introduction of such systems in Norwegian newspapers. Strikes have been organized against such systems in London, New York and Copenhagen.

(c) Industrial robots

Norway: one lifting robot, four programmed machine tools and one operator replace four skilled workers. (*Jernindustri*, no. 2, 78).

West Germany, Volkswagen: automatic welding robots were used cost efficiently in the production in 1978 (77 units). In 1980 such a robot can be operated at a cost of approximately £3 per hour and performs a lot more than a worker.

Volvo, Torslanda (Gothenburg) has reduced its workforce by 1200–1500 over the last few years. At the body-building factory, the workforce has been reduced from 1030 to 60 owing to the employment of welding robots.

(d) Teleautomation

More than 2000 jobs have been axed in Norway from 1964 to 1973 (automatic telephone exchanges) (Korbøl, 1977). The number of employees at L. M. Ericson (manufacture of telephone exchanges) was reduced from 15 000 in 1975 to 10 000 in 1978 with the same volume of production. This is largely due to automation of production. The number of workers was reduced from 8000 to 3000 during the period, whereas the number of salaried staff remained constant at 7000 (RDF, 1980).

Siemens's new all-electronic telephone exhanges are assembled in about 17 thousand hours of work, as opposed to about 99 thousand hours with the former design.

The telecommunication system which are to be introduced in England in the 1980s (system X), only requires an estimated 10 per cent of today's employees for production and maintenance work (RDF, 1980).

(e) To replace mechanics and electromechanics generally

Manufacture of watches: the south-western part of West Germany: 1970 – 32 000 employees; 1977 – 18 000 employees, owing to a change-over to electronic quartz watches and a reduced share of the market. Although the sales of watches have gone up in the world as a whole, estimates indicate a reduced number of employees in watch production (Freeman and Curnow, 1978).

Cash registers, a change-over to electronic models for NCR in the USA, reduced the manning in the production department from 37 000 in 1970 to 18 000 in 1977 (*Sunday Times,* 17 September 1978).

Taximeters (Kinzle): mounting time for an old mechanized model is 11.7 hours, whereas the new electronic one is mounted in 3.7 hours.

Admittedly, this list represents the most dramatic examples from a development which so far has lasted for 5–15 years. Other examples could easily have been produced, but this 'rattling off' should be sufficient to illustrate that in wholesale and retail trade, manufacturing and the office sector there are examples of relatively large negative impacts on employment and a high increase in productivity resulting from the introduction of EDP. The question is whether these consequences will remain unique examples in the 1980s.

3.2 General points about EDP in an enterprise

The use of EDP in an enterprise may have many consequences like improved control and survey of the production, new products or services and improved competitive ability. In an employment perspective, it is natural to put the emphasis on EDP as a means of rationalization. Up to the present, this also appears to be the most significant single application of data technology in the enterprises.

When attempting to describe general features of rationalization with EDP in enterprises, there are *no* features that necessarily occur in all instances of rationalization based on EDP. The variations in application and extent are too large for that. On the other hand, there are common features of such rationalization which occur so frequently that they are worth a closer description. Three such characterstics will be mentioned here, and they can be regarded as idealized descriptions of, or rather hypotheses on, impacts of EDP in an enterprise.

The first common feature is the occurence of sharper dividing lines between jobs. If an enterprise is regarded as a job hierarchy, it is obvious that EDP is not used in the same way throughout this hierarchy. The manager will not use EDP in the same way as those working on the shop floor. The 'top' jobs (top management, experts etc.) will assume more responsibility and control. Leaders on the middle and lower levels (group leaders, foremen) are to a large degree replaced by the EDP system, and the 'lowest' jobs tend to become less independent. The work here is to a large extent directed and controlled by the EDP systems.

As a consequence, there will be a wider gap between the 'top' and 'bottom' jobs. This is because the EDP systems, which replace the control previously performed by the lower management, transfer this control to higher levels of the organization. Rigid EDP systems and stronger control from the management thus lead to a more directed working situation for those working in production. This feature was also discovered in the investigation referred to in the next section of the article.

The second common feature which often appears, is that tasks which previously constituted *one* job are divided into two or more specialized jobs with clearly defined tasks, in accordance with nearly the same principle as for traditional mechanization. When this division has been completed, an EDP system can be devised, which replaces most or all of each part of the task. In order to design an EDP system, one needs a clear description of the tasks which are to be transferred to EDP. As the last step in this automation process, the separate parts which have been automated can be joined, by means of EDP, to make a complete system. Thereby people working with the transferring of information from one EDP system to another, will become redundant. The last step often appears to be far more difficult than the automation of each part of the task, but labour saving is normally highest here. It usually takes several years to realize such all-automation.

One example of this is office work, which over the years has developed specialized jobs like invoices, salaries and wages, files, accounting, typing etc. For each of these tasks, there is being, or has already been, made EDP systems which replace a lot the manual work. The idea behind what is called the office of the 1980s ('paperless office') is to have an automatic connection between these subsystems by means of EDP. Other examples of such division, partial automation and connection are to be found in printing and allied industries and mechanical industry.

The third feature, which seems to be particularly common in larger organizations using EDP, is that the use of EDP starts centrally with a relatively large computer. This installation could be shared among several enterprises in the form of a data processing centre. Step by step, EDP is brought out to the end-user. Banking is one example where joint central computers were used, into which data were punched and output received in the form of data listing. The first advance towards the user is to supply the counter clerks with a terminal where they record data and have output direct on the screen. Normally, the counter clerks will be just as busy after this innovation, but those who previously were punching data become redundant. The next step is to install automatic bank machines outside the bank premises in order that the customers can cash money themselves. The next step to bring EDP to the users, is to give the customers the opportunity to transfer money from their own bank account by way of the TV set at home, which is connected with the bank's computer through the telephone. Such services are now being tried out in France. It will also become possible to equip shops with automatic payment machines. When a customer inserts a bank card into such a machine, the machine will see that the amount to be paid is drawn from the customer's account and transferred to that of the shop. This application, in the form of payment for petrol sold in the Shell and Exxon petrol stations in Norway, is about to be introduced. Here, the fundamental principle used in order to automate is that data should only be recorded once. Instead of the customer first giving data to the counter, the counter to the punching department and the punching department to the computer, the whole procedure is reduced to the customer communicating direct with the computer. A lot of today's types of transactions (like bills, orders, general forms of payment) are handled on several levels without anything else taking place than simple and well-defined conversion of the content.

Finally, it has to be underlined that these features have been presented in an idealized way. The development in the use of EDP in the enterprises is full of contrasts, and such general features may be overshadowed by special conditions in the enterprise making use of EDP. Perhaps other features will appear to be typical in the 1980s, either in addition to or as a replacement of what has been mentioned above.

3.3 Experience from the municipality of Sandefjord and STK

At the Norwegian Computing Centre, an investigation of EDP in the office sector has been conducted during the last year (Espeli and Maus 1981a). In

addition to general studies of literature on the subject, the project has investigated:

(a) a larger stock control systems at Standard Telefon og Kabelfabrikk, the
    Teledivision. STK, which is the Norwegian subsidiary of ITT, employs
    about 3000 people, half of whom are salaried staff (Espeli and Maus 1981b);

(b) the total use of EDP in the central administration in the municipality of
    Sandefjord — with about 1100 employees, of whom 60 work in the central
    administration (Espeli and Maus, 1981c).

These two examples are rather dissimilar. On the one hand, there is the large
industrial which administers gradually fewer manual workers (because of automation in production) and on the other hand a medium-sized public administration which administers an increasing staff in service jobs. What is more, the
STK system represented an older EDP system with punch cards and a lot of
output on paper, whereas Sandefjord had a modern system based on screens and
data base. The processes of developing the systems were also totally dissimilar.
At STK the system had been developed by experts at the data processing department, while at the various departments of the central administration in Sandefjord,
some of the employees involved had developed and programmed their own
systems. They managed to do so because the tools for program design that were
at their disposal were specially devised for the ordinary users to design EDP
systems themselves. And that proved to be possible only after a few weeks of
training.

In spite of these differences, we discovered general agreement as regards the
following four conclusions.

(1) *Office automation with EDP pays.* It can for example be mentioned that
from 1969 to 79 the annual increase in productivity for the staff involved (about
35) at STK, was 8.5 per cent. This is nearly double the average increase for all
employees at STK (4.4 per cent), and more than fourfold the increase for the
salaried staff as a whole (2.0 per cent). A follow-up investigation of this project
indicated an internal rate of return on invested funds of about 60 per cent per
year. During the period 1969—79 the total sales (adjusted to inflation) have
increased by 35 per cent while the number of employees has increased from
3009 in 1969 to 4086 in 1972, only to decline to 3298 in 1979. The management as well as the employees mainly ascribe this reduction in employment
since 1972 to the use of EDP-assisted automation in production and office
work.

In Sandefjord the manning in the central administration has remained
constant (about 60 employees) since 1968, despite the fact that working expenses
and the number of municipal employees have nearly doubled during this period.

(2) *The profits of rationalization will not be collected immediately, but over several years.* They will be gradually collected (say over 3 to 10 years after the system has been introduced) because no-one is dismissed by the introduction, and therefore one has to await:

(a) natural retirement;
(b) growth in the amount of traditional tasks;
(c) introdution of new services or tasks to 'collect' the profits of rationalization. (Therefore the profits of rationalization will be difficult to assess).

(3) The number of lower employees stagnates (or declines), lower management is to a large extent made redundant (by the EDP system) and the number of top staff shows a substantial increase. Total employment levelled out in the offices that we studied, despite a relatively heavy increase in the amount of tasks.

(4) A demand seems to be created for extra manning of highly qualified employees (not only EDP experts) when an EDP system is being introduced. But this demand 'disappears' when the system seems relatively stable. But total organization effects of such new policies, like the employment of these relatively highly qualified co-workers, may be long-lasting. Disparity may easily occur between these new experts, mostly recruited from outside, and the old staff.

It has to be stressed that this project looked at management information systems where EDP has replaced manual routines (STK and Sandefjord) or older EDP systems (Sandefjord). These systems now perform what previous systems or routines did and provide in addition a good deal of new information/reports. Examples of systems that we had a look at are book-keeping of stocks, price calculation of compound products (telephone exchanges), purchasing routines, book-keeping, wage systems and technical information systems (registers of real estate etc.).

The project did not consider general systems for office automation like text processing, electronic mail, filing etc. However, we did not discover any rudiments of the 'paperless office'. At the place we visited, clear-cut separate tasks had been automated. But the number of such systems was large at both places, and people were not reluctant to accept the idea of integrating some of these at a later stage.

4 ELEMENTS OF TOTAL PERSPECTIVE

When trying to draw more general conclusions about the impacts of EDP on employment, it is absolutely necessary to draw on a general knowledge about what can be termed 'the labour market' and the effect of EDP in relation to all other factors believed to cause unemployment. Considerations of space makes it impossible to give but a short outline of today's knowledge in this field. But such a brief going through will at least make us understand that EDP is only *one* factor in the employment question (some writers seem to forget the fact that unemployment is a far older phenomenon than EDP). Nevertheless, this outline will give us the opportunity to draw some tentative conclusions.

4.1 The labour market

The first thing to be mentioned, is that the heading of this section is incorrect. There is not one, but a lot of labour markets in a society.

People have varying education, unequal occupational experience and live in different places. It is obvious that in your local environment there is only a limited number of jobs you can get if they become vacant. You easily become aware of that when looking through vacancies in a larger newspaper. Employment officers estimate that boys choose from approximately 300 occupations when going out to work, whereas girls in fact only choose from approximately 60 occupations. It is also important to note that it is not enough to have relevant education and live at the right place. One also has to be the best qualified applicant for the particular job. If one is too old or lacks occupational experience, has little formal education, has had problems with alcohol, is a foreign worker, has been sentenced or is a woman, one tends to end up at the back of the queue when applying for a job. If a person has too many 'negative' characteristics, like the ones mentioned above, experience shows that some employers often want a vacancy to remain unfilled rather than employ a person who is 'little productive'. One becomes excluded from the 'labour market'.

When looking at occupational categories in Norway, history shows the tendencies illustrated in Fig. 1. (source: Rasmussen, 1975). Figures showing the distribution of employees (in somewhat greater detail) are given in Table 2.

Table 2

1.	Agriculture and fishing	9.1%
2.	Manufacturing	20.3%
3.	Contract construction and transport	19.7%
4.	Trade, banking etc.	20.4%
5.	Public administration, education, health	25.8%
6.	Other activities	4.7%

(Source: Central Bureau of Statistics, *Monthly Bulletin*, 1/80.)

In 1979, 1.8 million people, or 46 per cent of the Norwegian population (about 65 per cent of those between the age of 16 and 74) were in paid empolyment. The occupational frequency for men is about 30 per cent higher than for women.

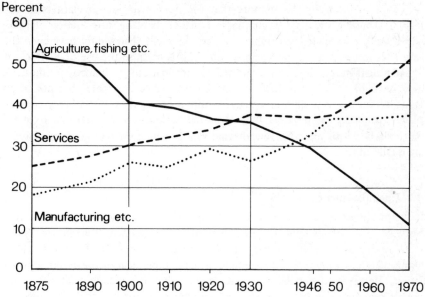

Fig. 1 – Economically active population by main groups of industry 1875–1970.

These statistics show, among other things, that the number of people employed in agriculture has strongly declined and that progressively more jobs have been created in the manufacturing and service industries. In most of the larger industrial countries, the number of jobs in the manufacturing industries has now strongly declined in the 1970s, and the increase in total employment has taken place in the service industry. This, to a certain extent, also applies to Norway. It is important to note that, since 1960, the number of jobs in public services, particularly education and health, has represented as much as 60 per cent of the increase in the number of jobs in Norway. (In 1980 about 25 per cent were employed in public services in Norway as opposed to 13 per cent in 1960). What are normally thought of as jobs, 'industrial work', only represent one-fifth of total employment. Therefore, one is on the wrong tack if one considers the total impacts of EDP on the basis of the impacts on industrial work or, for example, office work. In fact, more than half of the employed population work neither at an office nor as industrial workers.

Another distinctive feature is the obvious trend towards more widespread part-time work in the 1970s. While the number of employees in the period 1972–78 increased by about 200 000, or 12 per cent the number of working hours has only increased by 1 per cent. Today a larger number of employees therefore perform the same number of hours' work, which indicates that the number of part-time employees has increased heavily. Primarily women occupy these new part-time jobs.

As a summing up, let us note that the number of labour markets is very high in a modern society. Technological change, like the introduction of EDP, will therefore have stronger impacts on employment than would have been the case if everybody could manage any job. This is because the use of EDP is not equally distributed, but affects particular occupations or lines of business. It may be right to say that EDP will be introduced 'everywhere', but not to an equal extent and not simultaneously. Within a certain labour market at a given place, technological progress may therefore seriously affect the employment, particularly if this place has few alternative jobs which the redundant empolyees are qualified for.

4.2 Unemployment

It is not altogether easy to assess the number of unemployed in a country like Norway – it depends how the term 'unemployed' is defined. If we include those who receive unemployment benefit, the answer is simple. In December 1980, about 30 000 people received such benefit, i.e. 1.6 per cent of the working population. However, this does not quite cover what is generally understood by unemployment. Youngsters leaving school who have not had their first job, are not entitled to unemployment benefit. Older employees who have received unemployment benefit for more than one year are usually transferred to disability insurance and are thereby excluded from these statistics. (From 1963 the number of people receiving disability insurance increased from 75 000 to about 160 000 although the retirement age was lowered in 1972). In addition, the employment authorities finance a series of temporary jobs and provide a series of short courses for occupational training and rehabilitation in typing, welding etc. At any given time, about ten to twenty thousand people are engaged in this activity.

When including people claiming to be out of work according to the Central Bureau of Statistics' manpower inquiries, the number is normally about 50 per cent higher than the number of people receiving unemployment benefit. In the third quarter of 1980, 40 000 or 2.1 per cent were unemployed.

On the other hand, if we are of the opinion that unemployment means that people who want work do not get it, the unemployment figures are considerably higher in Norway. The Central Bureau of Statistics' manpower inquiries also give a survey of how many would go into work if suitable work was available nearby and if the conditions generally were favourable (nursery school etc.). In autumn 1980, another 110 000 were discovered in addition to the 40 000 claiming to be out of work and approximately 20 000 in retraining courses etc. With this definition of unemployment, about 170 000 or 8.9 per cent appear to be unemployed in Norway.

The largest part of this last group are housewives who want to go back to work, but who have no opportunities where they live, or older workers who have been put on disability insurance because no work can be found for them. They want work, but have largely given up seeking.

In Norway today it would make sense to estimate an unemployment rate of about 2–9 per cent. When comparing with other countries, the measuring method which gives an unemployment of about 10 per cent in Great Britain in 1981, gives nearly 3 per cent in Norway.

A lot of factors contribute to unemployment. They can be divided into the following four categories:

— trade depression;
— frictional problems;
— structural problems;
— a gap between economic growth and increase in productivity.

The first two categories are temporary whereas the two last ones are long-term problems.

Today's economic crisis and the ensuing unemployment are often described as a trade depression, i.e. declining demand for various goods and services. Few people will mention EDP as a cause of this declining demand. (If this is correct, it is obvious that the blame for most of today's unemployment cannot be ascribed to EDP.)

Frictional unemployment occurs when people are to change jobs. If one becomes redundant at one place, it will usually take some time until there is an offer for a new job — retraining and moving may be necessary. Even if the number of vacancies is equal to the number seeking employment, there will always be a pool of unemployment. As explained before, EDP can increase frictional unemployment by increasing the speed of reorganization in the economic life.

Structural problems are a more long-term maladjustment in the business structure. An example of this is the reorganization which has been necessary in the textile and ready-made clothing industries in Norway as a result of import from so-called cheap countries like Portugal, India and Hong Kong. EDP technology has already created such a structural problem: the world's watch production has largely been moved from Switzerland and West Germany to Japan, USA and Taiwan.

The three above-mentioned causes of unemployment mainly describe transitional problems, either due to a temporary maladjustment in the labour markets or a temporary shortfall in turnover and thereby a decline in employment. However, the most important question when discussing EDP and employment, is whether EDP will increase productivity at a higher speed than the growth of the economy and the supply of new employees. In other words: will automation proceed at a higher speed than the rise in total turnover and result in a larger and *lasting* disproportion between the number of jobs in society and the number of people seeking employment? This statement of the problem is highly controversial. If this is a possible turn of the events, and the progressively increasing worldwide unemployment does not seem to contradict this, EDP could, under certain circumstances, be a technology likely to cause such a disproportion.

This brief survey of the main categories of factors generally causing unemployment, indicates that possible negative impacts of EDP are long-term rather than short-term. However, it must be underlined that this survey does not give the slightest indication of the extent of the impacts possibly created by EDP. Experience shows that to predict the extent of unemployment is a complicated matter. In Great Britain, predictions concerning the situation in twelve months' time show variations in estimates of several hundred thousand. Therefore statements on what will happen over a period of five to ten years ought not to be supplied with figures.

4.3 EDP and employment – attempt at a summary

When trying to sum up total impacts that EDP may have on employment, it would be appropriate to go back to the point of departure of this article – a data-technological approach to the problem. Has this aspect made it possible for us to come up with an unequivocal answer? I am afraid not. This does not necessarily imply that the point of departure was wrong or unsuitable. An obvious advantage of this approach is the survey of present and future applications, the speed of introduction of the various applications, and the total amount of EDP in present use. Such insight is normally wanting when everything is seen from a sociological point of view or in the perspective of political economy. The weakness of our approach is the failure to fully understand the nature and dimension of the impacts on total employment.

From our point of view, we find that the development is not unambiguous, but full of contrasts. Even though there are a lot of tendencies predicting larger problems in the labour markets, there are also trends going in the other direction. Typically enough, the speed in the introduction of EDP in a certain line of business is slower than what is the impression one is left with when reading literature on the subject. But on the other hand, the number of various applications increases at a faster rate than most people are able to imagine. Despite this confusing picture, it seems possible to draw the following two conclusions.

First of all, we will most likely have more widespread unemployment problems than previously, because EDP will cause people to change occupation and job more frequently than before. A lot of occupations and types of education will no longer be current because the tasks have been transferred to EDP. Even if work is available in other industries or occupations, retraining and moving will cause problems. A lot of people will be too old or unfit for retraining and moving and will have to retire early. Those who manage to find a new job will perhaps not be out of work for too long. However, the problem has a long-term character, because progressively more and new application of EDP will be used on a large scale in the years to come.

Secondly, we find that the question whether EDP could create a larger and lasting unemployets problem, cannot be answered with a clear yes or no. The situation is rather that the (economic) policy to be conducted in the 1980s will give the answer. The possible impacts of EDP on employment will become so important that they require a political response.

There obviously seems to be certain political measures which could create vast unemployment. But it is equally obvious that other measures could avert this unemployment (for example a reduction of the working hours). Therefore it is of crucial importance what policy the trade unions, the employers and the political parties are going to choose. What data technology to apply and how to design the EDP systems are not determined or defined by technology. There is a freedom of choice within wide limits. EDP is a general technology which allows a wide choice as regards the degree of application and actual system design. The choice made will give the answer to questions about EDP and employment.

REFERENCES

CIS (1979) *The New Technology*, Counter Information Services, London.

Espeli and Maus (1981a) *Edb og sysselsetting i kontorsektoren* (EDP and employent in offices), Norwegian Computing Centre, Oslo (in Norwegian).

Espeli and Maus (1981b) *MASIS-prosjektet pa STK* (The MASIS project at STK), Norweigian Computing Centre, Oslo (in Norwegian).

Espeli and Maus (1981c) *Edb i Sandefjord kommune* (EDP in the municipalley of Sandefjord), Norwegian Computing Centre, Oslo (in Norwegian).

Freeman and Curnow (1978) *Technical Change and Employment – a Review of post-war research,* Science Policy Research Unit, University of Sussex, England.

Gershuny (1978) *After Industrial Society, The Emerging Self-service Economy,* MacMillian, London.

Halvorsen (1980) *Datateknikkens sosiale konsekvenser innen bankvesent* (The social consequences of data technology in banking), NAVF, Oslo (in Norwegian).

Korbøl (1977) *Teleautomatisering i etterkrigtida* (Telephone automation after World War II), Inst. for samfunnsforskning, Oslo (in Norwegian).

NOU 10 (1980) *Langtidsplan for Televerket* (Long-range plan for Norwegian PTT) Universitets forlaget, Oslo (in Norwegian).

Noyce (1977) Microelectronics, *Scientific American,* September, 1977.

Rada (1980) *The Impact of Micro-electronics,* ILO, Geneva.

Rasmussen (1975) Yrkesbefolkningen i Norge (The occupational people of Norway), Statistisk Sentralbyra, Oslo (in Norwegian).

RDF (1980) *80-tallet pa en bricka* (The 1980s on a chip), Riksdataforbundet, Stockholm (in Swedish).

Statistisk Senstralbyrå *Statistisk månedshefte og Arbeids markedsstatistikk*, 1972–80 (Statistical monthly and statistics of working market, 1972–80), Oslo (in Norwegian).

Working with visual display units

Kari Thoresen

1 INTRODUCTION

The use of visual display terminals has become an important issue over the last few years. This is partly because terminal work stations are becoming more common in offices, and partly because it is evident that such jobs create physical as well as psychological problems. Attempts are often made to solve the problems by improving the physical arrangement of the work station, involving the desk, the chair, the display unit and keyboard. However, one soon discovers that such measures only have limited effects. Probably, physical strain will be somewhat reduced. But it is far too narrow an approach to consider work only as a question of avoiding physical strain.

Certainly, there are many badly designed work stations in the physical sense, which should be improved. In Section 3.2 such problems and some of their answers are dealt with.

The Norwegian Working Environment Act, however, outlines a considerably wider concept of work, stressing the opportunities for professional as well as personal learning and development. This aspect of work is not notably influenced by the physical arrangement of the work-place.

Therefore, a perspective which is limited to the work station itself, limits our understanding of the problems which exist. We have to broaden the perspective and realize that a work station and the work performed there is part of a work unit, which again is embedded in a larger unit: a company or an organization. When focusing on the work station alone, we are left with only a partial view of reality. Causal relations are severed, and we are unable to fully understand which factors contribute to better working conditions with visual display units. Reduction of the workload may be more important than improved lighting, and the opportunity to alternate between different tasks may mean more than having displays with black characters on a white background. When discussing terminal work stations and working environment, it is important to bear in mind that they are part of a larger whole, and the method of approach must be adjusted accordingly.

This wider interpretation of the concept of working with VDUs forms the basis of this article. It draws on experience gained during the Norwegian Computing Centre's projects on the working environment and visual display terminals (1977–1980), including a literature survey and an empirical investigation on various jobs involving terminals.

The aim was as follows:

(1) to establish criteria of good and bad VDU work stations;
(2) to build up knowledge about working conditions at various types of VDU work;
(3) to formulate the VDU operators' demands and requests concerning equipment, systems design and job arrangement.

The empirical investigation involved six different work-places with 113 employees altogether. Different jobs were included, such as data entry, text processing, travel bureau services, order entry and other activities involving customers.

The Working Environment Act, and Section 12 in particular, is the basis of our investigation. The sections in question will be discussed in further detail in Section 3.1 here in. Other agreements, for example the General Agreement on Computer-based Systems, also provide possibilities for tackling these issues. But our work has been based on the wording of and the intentions behind the Working Environment Act.

The project findings are presented in two reports: 'Terminal work stations' and 'Working conditions with VDUs'.

Our investigations leave us with the impression that working conditions fall far short of the requirements of Section 12. Most of the jobs provide few opportunities for professional and personal development, with the exception of a short period after the introduction of the VDUs. Both technology and the organization of work are factors causing physical strain. Among the employees 70–80 per cent suffer from eye strain, aching muscles, tiredness and headache after most of the day at a VDU. People using the VDU for short periods, and for less than a couple of hours a day, are considerably less affected.

The physical working environment is often unsatisfactory at most places. However, it is encouraging to see that many organizations are working to improve conditions.

Possibilities for contact with others are usually good, particularly for those staff dealing with customers. But owing to an increasing work load, the time spent with each customer is reduced. The data processing system is also a controlling factor, particularly when poor operating performance creates an unstable working situation.

Our investigation indicates that better physical working conditions together with a reorganization of work, will improve jobs to a larger extent than relying exclusively on better equipment and facilities.

Facts and conclusions presented in this chapter are collected not only from our two reports, but also from other investigations from the past few years. It is rarely possible to make direct comparisons between such research projects. There are different approaches to the problems, and methodologies vary. But together they convey a picture of office work with VDUs which shows that problems cannot be solved by simple means.

2 VDU WORK – SOME CENTRAL CONCEPTS

2.1 Approach

Our description of working with VDUs is related to the familiar description of organization charts. The organization is divided into departments and further divisions within the departments, with the job, the individual and the data processing equipment as basic units. This is a simplified description of an organization, which would not be adequate for an understanding of an organization in a wider perspective. It may, however, be useful for showing the relationship between many of the requirements of the Working Environment Act and the reality which a VDU operator experiences daily.

Some of the central concepts used in this chapter, will be discussed under this heading. They do not necessarily apply to all types of office jobs. Other investigations suggest that departmental and work organization differ considerably in other office environments (Baadshaug, 1980, and Wynn 1979).

2.2 Concepts and examples

An assumption is made that VDU work stations are to be found in a *department* of a company or an organization. Every department may be divided into sections, but in our case each department has been allocated one particular function, for example data entry, text processing, order entry etc. We have chosen this somewhat limited concept of a department because it reflects a pattern common to the places we visited, not because we think it is ideal. On the contrary, such a structure may hamper efforts to change working conditions.

Within each department there is a set of tasks which are distributed among several jobs. A *job* includes a combination of tasks, responsibility and authority, often attached to a particular person. The job may be static, or it may change by new tasks, responsibility and authority being added. Our job concept differs from that expressed in every-day language – e.g. 'we have a big job in front of us', where job denotes a strong effort within a certain time limit; it is an all-out effort which may well be exerted by a lot of people.

Work is organized according to a pattern which includes the arrangement of jobs and their distribution between different persons over a period of time. This pattern will be termed *work organization*. The organization of work may vary from one department to another, and will also, over a period of time, vary within each department. At a text processing centre, for example, the work may be organized so that each person is responsible for the clerical work of one other department in the company. The main responsibilities are to communicate with the department, write and correct manuscripts, and hand them to the right persons. The job involves personal responsibility for the tasks performed, and authority to determine or change delivery dates, and if necessary alter the layout of manuscripts and work priority.

Alternatively, a supervisor may be responsible for communication with user departments and allocates assignments to the operators in the text processing centre. The supervisor's job is to cooperate with the rest of the company, to plan the work of the operators, to see that they are working, and to control their performance. She has to account for work being done within the appointed time, and she has the authority to decide the allocation of manuscripts and time limits. As opposed to the first example, responsibility and authority is centralized, and the work is more unevenly distributed among the different levels of the text processing centre, compared with the first example.

Jobs are usually arranged in a hierarchy with a supervisor at the top. In a hierarchical work organization, the supervisor is in charge of planning, distribution and control of work. The operators do the practical work. Other categories of work organization may have a more flexible distribution of planning and performance.

A department is located at a particular work place, i.e. premises with particular furniture, lighting, noise level etc. A *work station* is part of a workplace where a VDU is frequently used in the work. A work station in this case includes a visual display unit with a keyboard, and possibly also a printer and storage devices like floppy disks. The work station also comprises furniture, such as a desk, chair or a counter. The VDU is used by one or more persons whom we call *VDU operators.*

By means of the VDU terminal the operator is connected to a *data processing system.* This may be on-line (interactive), or batch processing, for example batch input or output on microfilm. In this chapter we will concentrate on interactive data processing systems used for various office functions. The function of these systems is determined by the nature of the work in different offices. We will only discuss dedicated systems, i.e. systems which can only carry out a particular set of tasks. One example is an order entry system, where a limited selection of goods can be ordered, stocks can be updated and invoices made out. Such systems may be distributed throughout the company, but the use of the system is specialized. One department deals with order entry, another with stock, and a third with invoices. At quite a few of the VDU terminals in our study, an important part of the work consists in rendering services to customers, usually across a counter or on the telephone. The role of the VDU terminal in the total picture strongly depends on the organization of work. The strain on the individual operator will vary with the time spent in front of the screen. If the VDU is used for short periods only, and other work is done in between, the strain is reduced. If used more or less continuously during the day, the demands for a high-quality work station increases.

3 THE WORKING ENVIRONMENT ACT

3.1 Important sections

In 1977 the Norwegian Working Environment Act was revised. The old version concentrated on the traditional worker protection strategies, mostly directed towards the typical problems in industrial work: dust, noise, chemicals etc. The new version also includes sections more relevant to office work (e.g. section 12), and points towards new ways of handling working environment problems, based on local activities.

Chapter I of the act specifies that:

The objectives of this Act are:

1. to secure a working environment which affords the employees full safety against harmful physical and mental influences and which has safety, occupational health and welfare standards that correspond to the level of technological and social development of the society at large at any time.

2. to secure sound contract conditions and meaningful occupation for individual employees,

3. to provide a basis whereby the enterprises themselves can solve their working environment problems in cooperation with the organizations of employers and employees and under the supervision and guidance of the public authorities.

The working Environment Act lays down requirements with regards to technical equipment, work organization and the employees right to participate. Some of the sections are particularly relevant to screen work, i.e. section 9, 'Technical apparatus and equipment', and section 12, 'Planning the work'.

Section 9 specifies that:

Technical apparatus and equipment in the enterprise shall be designed and provided with safety devices so as to protect employees from injury and disease.

When technical apparatus is being installed and used, care shall be taken to ensure that the employees are not exposed to undesirable effects from noise, vibrations, uncomfortable working positions etc.

Technical apparatus and equipment should be designed and installed so that it can be operated by or be adapted for use by employees of varying physique.

Technical apparatus and equipment shall always be maintained and attended.

Section 12 specifies first the general requirements:

Technology, organization of the work, working hours and wage systems shall be set up so that the employees are not exposed to undesirable physical or mental strain and so that their possibilities of displaying caution and observing safety measures are not impaired.

Conditions shall be arranged so that employees are afforded reasonable opportunity for professional and personal development through their work.

secondly about the arrangement of work:

The individual employee's opportunity for self-determination and professional responsibility shall be taken into consideration when planning and arranging the work.

Efforts shall be made to avoid undiversified, repetitive work and work that is governed by machine or conveyor belt in such a manner that the employees themselves are prevented from varying the speed of the work. Otherwise efforts shall be made to arrange the work so as to provide possibilities for variation and for contact with others, for connection between individual job assignments, and for employees to keep themselves informed about production requirements and results.

VDU terminals must be used in such a manner that they contribute to an improvement of the factors mentioned above. Moreover, the supplement to section 12 is very restrictive with regard to recording of individual work effort.

The supplement also stresses the importance of employees' opinions. There is no need for expert statements to decide whether the work is tedious or the work load too heavy.

The employees' right to participate is dealt with in section 12.3: 'Control and planning systems', which specifies that:

The employees and their elected union representatives shall be kept informed about the systems employed for planning and effecting the work, and about planned changes in such systems. They shall be given the training necessary to enable them to learn these systems, and they shall take part in planning them.

Section 14, 'Duties of the employer' specifies:

The employer shall ensure that the enterprise is arranged and maintained, and that the work is planned, organized and performed in accordance with the provisions stipulated in or by virtue of this Act, see in particular Sections 7–13.

To ensure that the safety, health and welfare of the employees is taken into consideration at all levels thoughout the enterprise, the employer shall:

(a) when planning new work-places, alteration of work-places or production methods, procurement of technical apparatus and equipment etc., study and evaluate whether the working environment will be in compliance with the requirements of this Act and effect the measures necessary;

(b) arrange continuous charting of the existing working environment in the enterprise as regards risks, health hazards and welfare, and effect the measures necessary;

(c) arrange continuous checks of the working environment and the health of employees when there may be a risk of health injuries caused by long-term effects from influences in the working environment;

(d) arrange for expert assistance and for testing and measuring equipment when this is necessary in order to comply with the requirements of the Act;

(e) organize and arrange the work giving due consideration to the age, proficiency, working ability and other capabilities of the individual employees;

(f) arrange for systematic promotion of safety within the enterprise, and ensure that qualified persons with an understanding of safety matters are appointed to ascertain that the work is performed in a proper manner as regards safety and health;

(g) ensure compliance with the provisions of the Act relating to systematic promotion of safety, see Chapter VII;

(h) ensure that employees are informed of any accident risks and health hazards that may be connected with the work and that they receive the necessary training, practice and instruction.

The supplement to Section 14 states that in the effort to improve the working environment, the employees' influence in the decision making process should be emphasized. Employees are to participate in investigations of the working environment as well as the design of improvement programmes. This right to participate applies to the individual employee, the safety delegate and the local working environment committee.

3.2 The practical consequences of the Act

Hardly anyone expects such legal requirements to be fully complied with. Besides, the Act merely provides general guidelines. It is up to the Labour Inspectorate and local working environment committees to define the actual contents of the Act. This work has just begun, and we will discuss the likely practical implication.

Requirements concerning terminal equipment

It is difficult to point out exactly which features or work stations create health injuries. Normally, health injuries are not caused by the equipment alone, but by a combination of equipment, surrounding, work organization and personal factors. Occurrence of skin rashes, also called 'the Norwegian disease' is a good example. Some employees developed facial rashes (Lindén, 1981), probably due to static electricity caused by high voltage in the cathode ray tube in the screen. People who are susceptible to such exposure may be affected if they sit too long in front of the screen. Conditions can be improved, for example by means of earthed antistatic carpets.

Noise is a problem which is almost only caused by printers and a few storage devices such as floppy disk stations etc. They produce different types of noise. Impact printers are particularly noisy when the hammers hit the sheet. A noise level of 75–80 decibels is not uncommon. Apart from this, noise is produced from fans in different parts of the equipment. This noise does not have a particularly high decibel level, but is annoying because of its continuity and its spectrum of sounds.

Another problem with screens is the generation of heat. This varies a lot, depending on how many printed circuit boards have been incorporated in the screen, i.e. its data processing capacity. We have observed variations from 35–500 W.

Screens may therefore be a considerable source of heat, particularly because they must remain on throughout the year, no matter how cold or warm the weather may be. Special consideration should therefore be given to ventilation and air conditioning.

Vibration is not a widespread problem, but may occur when heavy equipment, for example a printer, is attached to a counter or a desk. The desk itself is sometimes so unstable that strokes on the keyboard may cause vibration.

An uncomfortable working position often results from the screen being too high or too low, or if the reading distance is wrong. To adjust the terminal to individual requirements, the screen and the keyboard must be separate, and the desk and chair adjustable. Otherwise, the inevitable result is a cricked neck and tense muscles in the arms and shoulders. There should also be an opportunity to vary the reading distance individually.

VDU operators commonly complain of headaches, trouble with eyes, neck, shoulders and, to a certain extent, the back. Fifty per cent report having three or more symptoms, sometimes or frequently. Less than 10 per cent report no symptoms (Ekenes and Thoresen, 1980). Muscle ailments are, however, a problem in many kinds of office work, and we do not know for certain whether VDU operators are particularly affected, although some investigations do indicate this (Hünting *et al*. 1980; Smith *et al*. 1980).

Hünting *et al*. (1980) found that 60 per cent of data-entry operators developed painful pressure points at tendons, joints and muscles in the area of shoulders (medical findings), while less than 10 per cent traditional office workers experienced the same. Self-reports on 'almost daily' pains in neck, shoulders, right arm and right hand also show high incidence in the data-entry group, and low in the control group of traditional office workers.

But it is too simple to put the blame on badly arranged work stations alone. The causes are to be found just as much in the organization of work, which is often tedious, strictly controlled and highly pressurized. Our investigation shows that those employees who have specialized in screen work and sit most of the day in front of a screen, are more likely to develop physical ailments than those who sit there for a short time every day (see Fig. 1).

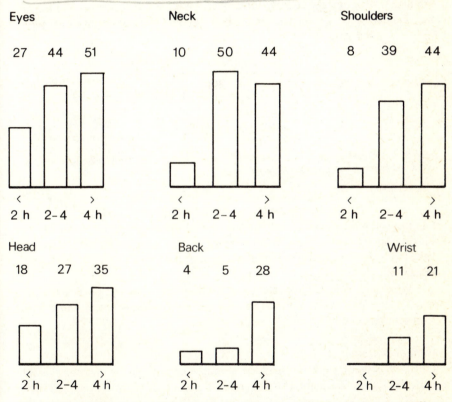

Fig. 1 – The relation between total time spent at the screen per day, and percentage suffering symptoms daily or several times a week.

This also agrees with the findings of a Swedish report (Johansson and Aronsson, 1979) showing that people's limit of tolerance for screen work (i.e. how long can one spend in front of the screen before feeling discomfort) is less than 1½ hours. Eighty per cent felt some sort of discomfort before 1½ hours had passed, usually eye strain, mental fatigue and headaches.

Eyesight particularly is affected by screen work, and it has been well documented that such work causes problems for a large percentage of screen operators (Gunnarson and Østberg, 1977; Dainoff, 1980; Laubli *et al.* 1980).

The symptoms vary, the most common ones are related to eye fatigue (pains, burning, red eyes) or blurred vision. Up to 70—80 per cent of the full-day screen operators report eye fatigue (Ekenes and Thoresen, 1980). This is considerably more than in traditional office work, although eye fatigue occurs here to — approximately 22 per cent report eye fatigue (Baadshaug, 1980).

To a certain degree the eye complaints depend on how the screen is used (see Fig. 2). Those who use the screen for information purposes (conversational terminals), which means actively looking at the screen, report more eye fatigue than the data entry group. The sample includes only full-day screen work, and is therefore rather small.

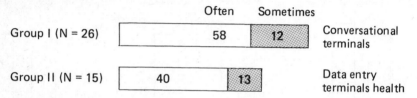

Fig. 2 — Differences in eye complaints for two types of work. Only full-day screen work included (Ekenes and Thoresen, 1980).

Some characteristics of the screen may contribute to this effect. The characters may be blurred, particularly on the edge of the display, and the display may flicker. An antiglare treatment is necessary to ensure minimum reflection from light fields in the room, like lamps, windows etc. Windows and light walls in the visual field may also cause contrast glare.

Personal factors are important too. Older people may not be able to focus quickly at close range, and people with ordinary bifocals will need different lenses for screen work.

Work organization

Considerations of work organization are more comprehensive and considerably more difficult to elucidate. Out research has considered the following factors:

— working hours and breaks;
— work load and manning levels;
— division of work and specialization;
— social contact and work-related contact;
— opportunity for control of work;
— training and in-service training;
— information and the right to participate.

These factors constitute an essential part of section 12, and are a prerequisite for a work organization which will give opportunities for professional and personal development. They also give an indication of what physical and mental strains are caused by such work.

The following comments are based on our own investigation, unless the contrary is stated. We refer to observed conditions, not necessarily discussing causal relations, i.e. whether the conditions are rooted in technology or other factors.

Working hours and breaks

Most of the places we visited have full-time working hours. About 10 per cent of the employees work part-time, i.e. they work a full day, but not a full week. Seventy per cent work 'flextime' and are very pleased with the arrangement. With such a high proportion of full-time employees, one has to expect a high level of physical ailments. Other investigations show that the part-time employees are spared some of the problems created by full-time work.

Arrangements for breaks are dealt with in two ways. Employees who mostly deal with customers, usually have a fixed lunch break, taken in turn. During the rest of the day, the stream of customers determines breaktimes. With the exception of the lunch break, employees may have to sit continously, or have irregular breaks. In some places the employees are free to take a five-minute break when they need it, but they usually refrain from doing so when the office is busy. In other cases, a short break in the morning and one in the afternoon have been arranged, provided the number of employees remaining is sufficient to deal comfortably with the work load. However, our main impression is that customer thoughput controls the break arrangements.

In the second category, employees do not handle customers in the previous sense. They have a better opportunity to arrange their working day. One way is to have fixed breaks for everybody, usually two short ones and a long one each day, with extensive work periods in between. Another way is to have fixed lunch breaks and shorter breaks according to individual needs. The last arrangement is probably most satisfactory, in order to avoid tiredness for the individual. on the other hand, the shorter breaks may be completely omitted on busy days.

Work load and manning levels

Most places considered themselves to be poorly manned, particularly in periods of heavy pressure of work. At some places the amount of work had increased, without new personnel being recruited. In some cases not even those who left were replaced. Our impression was that the average work load had increased.

It is difficult to measure work load, partly because strain is perceived in various ways by different people. When questioned about tiredness after work and whether the pressure of work was too high, 75–80 per cent answer 'sometimes' or 'often'.

Division of work and specialization

A majority of the departments are highly specialized. In the data entry department, everyone enters data. In the telephone sales department, everyone deals with order entry. This limits the possibility of creating varied jobs. But even in specialized departments, the work can be arranged to vary the content. Extremes are to be found in the hierarchical and non-hierarchical models.

In the hierarchical department, the supervisor plans and inspects the work, communicates with outsiders and performs the most advanced tasks. What is left for the operators, is the routine and monotonous part of the work. They have few opportunities to learn and develop new skills, and gradually quite a few become afraid of taking on more challenging jobs. This creates a vicious circle where the gap between the top and the lower levels of the department widens. In addition the working conditions of the operators increase the health hazard.

In the non-hierarchical department everyone is, to a large extent, capable of performing most of the jobs within the department. Tasks are rotated, normally according to a scheme worked out by the employees themselves. The role of the supervisor, if there is one, is less specialized, and she usually takes part in practical work. Responsibility and authority is distributed evenly throughout the department. Such an arrangement has positive advantages: people meet new challenges and learn new things, such as solving new problems and carrying responsibility and authority.

Our investigation does not cover the extremes on this scale, but the departments researched represent a major part of the spectrum in Table 1. We have divided the departments into two groups: 'hierarchical' and 'non-hierarchical', and asked the employees how they view their opportunities to learn and, whether their work is interesting or monotonous.

Table 1

	Percentage answering yes	
	Hierarchical	Non-hierarchical
Do you think there is more to learn?	24	50
Do you think the job is interesting?	19	55
Do you think the job is monotonous?	65	45

However, a hierarchical work organization is only one of the factors contributing to monotony and over-specialization. A less tangible but no less important factor, is pressure of work. To do jobs as quickly as possible, the employees 'voluntarily' organize division of work. Everyone does what she is good at, and the opportunities for variation and learning are reduced.

Contact with others

Opportunities for personal contact vary considerably between employees dealing with customers and those who do not. In the data entry department and the text processing centre, contact within the group is good, but the groups are isolated. Therefore, they lose the chance of seeing the part they play in the company, thus making it difficult to understand the total working procedures. Less than 10 per cent of the staff in the data entry departments and the text processing centre had a good knowledge of working procedures in the company as a whole, as opposed to 50 per cent in other departments.

The contact pattern for those dealing with customers, is considerably more varied. But this pattern is in the process of changing towards a more impersonal and formal contact. Heavier pressure of work results in less time available for each customer, and communications must be adapted to the requirements of the computer system. Another factor is that telephone contact is being replaced by message switching on the VDU, something which most people regret.

Control of work

This section considers the employee's opportunity to arrange her own work, as regards speed, work priority and how to perform the tasks.

At most of the places studied, the work is to a large extent directed by the stream of customers and by established routines. In addition, the computer system itself is a controlling factor. Not that it determines the working speed in the same way as an assembly line: nor is salary determined by the work speed. This may be the case in piecework, as for example in data entry, but that was not practised in our cases. Control is of a less tangible kind. There is a new dependence, and an implicit demand to use the equipment in an efficient way.

One of the factors creating dependence, is unreliable operating performance. Machine breakdowns tend to cause uneven work load, hamper dealing with customers and interrupt schedules. Poor reliability is frequently considered to be one of the major stress factors in such work.

Other aspects of work may be influenced too. The pace of work often has to be adjusted to response times, and the system may interrupt work to give messages, status reports etc. Some of the controlling factors do not only affect the working conditions of employees, but will have consequences for customers too.

Ordering routines are defined by the system, and previous flexibility towards customers is reduced, thereby lowering the service level.

Performance measurements are incorporated in some of the systems studied. The way such information is used varies from place to place. Sometimes it is ignored and sometimes used for strict control of individual performance. The latter occurs even though the Work Environment Act warns against such measurements, and despite the fact that the principles for such measurements give a false picture of work activity.

Training and in-service training

The amount of training varies considerably from one place to another. Most of the employees have attended a 3—5 day course, often provided by the machine vendor. The courses are not always satisfactory, and this gives the impression that training is a matter of secondary importance in most organizations. Only the travel agency is satisfied with employees' basic training, which lasts longer and has been developed over several years.

The situation leaves a great deal to be desired. Often the training given has not been adjusted to particular tasks, or it lacks thoroughness. And as a rule the training only provides the minimum of instruction necessary to operate the system, without giving users an understanding of the system in general.

The practical course arrangements are not always satisfactory either. Frequently there are too few terminals for individual practice and the 'training' deteriorates into a demonstration. The period of training must be coordinated with the introduction of equipment: neither too early nor too late.

Two of the places studied, the text processing centre in particular, have participated in the systems design. This, to a certain degree, explains why these work-places clearly differ from the rest regarding the employees' knowledge of their own system. Such understanding is not automatically acquired through extensive use of the system, unless certain conditions are present. These conditions are related to the character of the work, its organization, and participation in the systems design.

If the work demands a thorough knowledge of the system and the data which is processed, such knowledge will gradually be acquired. The same thing applies to the organization of work. The more limited your work and your field of responsibility are, the less you understand of your own work and the processing of data. This has obvious effects on the individual's job satisfaction, and the quality of the work produced.

4 CHANGES IN OFFICE WORK

Traditionally the office has been regarded as a pleasant work-place, with few working environment problems. There are no traditional 'factory floor' problems, like noise and dust pollution, heavy lifts and dangerous operations etc. And there are still reasons to believe that offices are in a better position than the factory as regards accidents and common occupational diseases.

However, we may question whether the general understanding of work environment factors is too heavily influenced by the traditional problems of the factory. This has been acknowledged in the Working Environment Act, where demands on the arrangement of work applies to offices at least as much as to other occupational categories. The incidence of physical and mental strain in office environments where visual display units are used, is partly a result of the organization of work and partly the design of work stations and equipment.

The fact that many operators experience health problems, has gradually been acknowledged and has resulted in various measures to evade the problem. There are tendencies to convert full-time jobs into part-time jobs, and to select people for VDU work.

Health problems in the form of muscle and eye trouble, headaches and tiredness, have now been documented by various investigations. Table 2 shows some of the Scandinavian investigations made during the past few years. Vifladt's investigation show that, on average, screen users have a higher frequency of eye troubles, headaches and tiredness. The same complaints also occur most frequently in the investigations without control groups.

But the picture is not unambiguous. In a series of investigations on job stress in VDU work Smith *et al.* (1980 and 1981) point out a number of factors contributing to the physical and psychological problems. Among these are job task-related features like job content, task requirements and work load. VDU operators reporting the highest level of stress and health complaints, worked according

Table 2

Percentage suffering from different symptoms daily or several times a week

	Ekenes and Thoresen $N = 113$	Gunnarson and Ostberg $N = 48$	Vifladt with VDUs $N = 339$	Vifladt without VDUs $N = 100$
Eyes				
tiredness	35	75	34–35[a]	19
smarting, itching	19		9–12	8
Neck				
stiffness	29	18	24–34	31
pain	19		16–28	25
Shoulders	27	12–54[b]	16–30	30
Back				
stiffness	9	32	13–20	19
pain	10		15–17	14
Wrists	10	6	6–10	12
Headache	25	6	22–27	19
Long periods of tiredness	35		21–28	19

[a] The two columns refer to two groups who use screens occasionally (to the left) and often (to the right).

[b] Refers to two different terms for shoulders in Swedish.

to 'rigid work procedures with high production standards, constant pressure for performance, very little operator control over job tasks, and little identification with and satisfaction from the end-product of their work activity'.

The interaction between job characteristics and VDU use is most clearly exposed when comparing professional and clerical VDU work. Smith *et al.* (1981) investigated professional VDU users who held jobs that 'allowed for flexibility, control over job tasks, utilization of their education, and a great deal of satisfaction in their end-product'. This group reported considerably fewer health complaints than the clerical operators, in fact they were more similar to the control group, except for eye strain, burning eyes and irritation.

Perhaps this explains why so many computer professionals regard the reports on VDU problems with scepticism. They use the VDUs as a tool in jobs with learning opportunities, high degree of freedom, variation and career possibilities. In short – their jobs fulfil the requirements of The Working Environment Act. They are free to arrange their working day in such a way as to minimize the physical strain.

In theory there should not be any obstacles to arranging screen work in a satisfactory way. But in practice there are a series of factors causing stress in these jobs.

Firstly the equipment is expensive. Therefore high demands are made on utilization of equipment, which is often achieved through specialization of tasks. It is predictable that such jobs are likely to create problems. Possibly, the demands for high utilization will decrease somewhat when equipment costs fall. But for the moment this is not the case. Sharing equipment is also a possibility but this normally creates queuing problems.

Secondly, there are some obvious features of VDU work which cause stress. The control factors mentioned in Section 3.2. indicate that the anticipation of system breakdowns resulted in a working rhythm which differed considerably from the control group, measured physiologically by the amount of stress hormones present (Johansson and Aronsson, 1979).

Thirdly, some kind of rationalization is normally expected when computer-based systems are introduced, either in the form of labour-saving or increased productivity with the same number of employees. This expectation, which usually is a result of marketing tactics, rather than accurate pilot studies may lead to increased working pressure on the operators.

There is also a tendency to offer certain types of screen work, like data entry, to part-time employees. Partly the reason may be that full-time employment in such work causes strain. But if this is going to be a way of 'solving' working environment problems, we are on to a dangerous development.

Another undesirable tendency, concerns the selection of VDU operators. Older people and those with minor eye defects, may have difficulties with adapting to work that places high demands on their eyes. EDP-analyzer (1977) suggests that operators at text processing centres should:

— prefer to work with machines rather than people;
— enjoy working with details;
— accept sitting in the same position for long periods;
— be able to work undisturbed by noise and other activities;
— be used to accurate control and correction of work.

Norway is probably well prepared to resist such principles of selection. The Work Environment Act states that working conditions are to be adjusted to people and not vice versa. This does not imply that one should insist on everybody's right to work with VDUs. Certainly, there are cases when it is for the good of everyone to offer terminal operators new jobs, if they no longer are able to cope with screen work. However, there is a considerable difference between using selection as a principle and as a last resort.

5 HOW TO SOLVE THE PROBLEMS

A number of conditions have to be fulfilled, before technology represents a positive contribution to the working environment for an office worker. One advantage is, however, that the topic has received a great deal of attention in the past few years. One should take advantage of this by using the introduction of office technology as a means of initiating a more extensive process of change in the working place.

The introduction of new data processing systems is an unstable period for an organization. Jobs and routines are changed, new information networks and competence are built up. This is a good starting point for developing new ways of organizing work. The Working Environment Act supports this course of action.

Therefore, it is important to make proper use of the Working Environment Act. Much of this activity must take place at the 'grass roots' level of the organization. The employer, the safety delegate and the shop stewards must ensure that screen operators participate in the process. Experience has shown that union representative who do not work with terminals themselves, have difficulty in seeing the real problems, and how they appear to the operators.

The Working Environment Act maps out methods that are different from earlier laws. Previous laws stressed the importantce of environmental tolerance limits which were laid down by the Government. Such tolerance limits are still an important part of the new Act in the form of more detail provisions. In addition, the Act provides a strategy for *changing jobs* in a participative process. In this process, standards and tolerance limits will be less important. The real challenge is to work out and introduce local solutions.

These two methods of approach are rather different. These differences are reflected in the time-span of implementation, and the impact on the participants.

Ensuring that occupational hygiene standards are followed at a working place is a 'time-limited' process which has relatively little impact on the employees. When the new ergonomically satisfactory equipment has been installed, the task is complete, with no further action needed. Discomfort, it is hoped is reduced. Beyond this, nothing has changed in the job or the individual.

To change the job, on the contrary, is a continuous process which takes time, and usually leads to a corresponding change in the individual and the group: in attitudes, learning, insight and experience. As a result, the employees will make new and different demands on the work. At the same time, the environment will make new demands concerning products and services. Technology opens up new possibilities, and the organization gradually takes on a new form. This process is not restricted in time, because a given work organization will only be suitable for a limited period in the history of the work-place. Therefore, it is impossible to establish detailed standards for a 'good' work organization. Each work-place has to develop its own, within the framework of the Working Environment Act.

This will be a difficult task in many organizations, partly because of highly specialized departments. Some improvements can be achieved by redistributing different tasks within a department. But since the tasks to be distributed are rather uniform, it is difficult to provide varied work for everyone. In that case, cooperation with other departments may be necessary to experiment with new arrangements. Preferably, these departments should be part of the same integrated work system as the VDU work, so that the employees may better understand the connection between their own work and the rest of company. This will break with the traditional specialized organisational structure, and may meet resistance from the employer as well as employees. But it is difficult to see ways to improve working conditions in specialized departments, without reorganizing on a larger scale.

One possible means is to reduce working hours at the screen, for example, to four hours per day. It would help reduce physical strain and encourage job redesign. The danger is, of course, that full-time jobs would be divided into several part-time jobs. Physical strain may be reduced that way, but simultaneously it reduces the possibilities for achieving some of the other objectives in section 12. Shorter periods at the screen should therefore be combined with a union policy which does not allow unlimited use of part-time work.

It has often been maintained, particularly among people in the computing field that the present problems are caused by old technology. When the cathode ray tube is replaced by flat screens which are moveable, with split-screen, graphics and colours, the problems will be eliminated.

Owing to lack of experience with this type of technology, this argument cannot be categorically rejected. But the argument carries less weight than people seem to think, for the following two reasons.

— Traditional CRT screens will be used in the majority of the VDU work stations for the next 5—10 years. They will play an important role in the daily life of most operators. The existence of advanced screens in research laboratories, for military purposes or special tasks, does not benefit all those who struggle with old technology.

– Only a few of the problems described are caused by technology alone. If modern screens are to improve working conditions, the introduction of these must be accompanied by a reorganization of work. The belief in technology as the only means to improve conditions, may at worst serve as an excuse for maintaining monotonous routine work.

Our research indicates good reasons for acting now, instead of pinning one's faith on technological progress alone.

REFERENCES

Baadshaug, M. B. (1980) Å arbeide på kontor. En undersökelse av miljö og arbeidsoppgaver (Office work. A study of tasks and working environment), Norsk Produktivitetsinstitutt, 163 pp. (in Norwegian).

Cakir, A., Hart, D. J. and Stewart, T. F. M. (1979) The VDT Manual, Inca-Fiej Research Corporation, 253 pp.

Dainoff, M. J. (1980) Visual fatigue in VDT operators, in E. Grandjean and E. Vigliani (eds.), Ergonomic Aspects of Visual Display Terminals, Taylor and Francis Ltd., London.

EDP-analyzer (1977) Word processing, Part II, vol. 15. no. 3.

Ekenes, A. and Thoresen, K. (1980) Arbeidsforhold med dataskjerm (Working conditions with VDUs), Norsk Regnesentral, nr. 665, 108 pp. (in Norwegian).

Gunnarsson, E. and Östberg, O. (1977) Fysisk och psykisk arbetsmiljö i et terminalbaserat datasystem (Physical and psychological work environment in a computer-based office system with terminals), Arbetarskyddstyrelsen, Arbetsmedicinska Avdelningen, AMMF (in Swedish).

Hünting, W., Läubli, Th., and Grandjean, E. (1980) Constrained postures of VDU operators, in E. Grandjean and E. Vigliani (eds.), Ergonomic Aspects of Visual Display Terminals, Taylor and Francis Ltd., London.

Johansson, G. and Aronsson, G. (1979) Stressreaktioner i arbete vid bildskärms-terminal, (Stress reactions working with screen terminals), Psykologiska Institutionen, Stockholms Universitet, 46 pp. (in Swedish).

Läubli, Th., Hünting, W., and Grandjean, E. (1980) Visual impairments in VDU operators related to environmental conditions, in E. Grandjean and E. Vigliani (eds.), Ergonomic Aspects of Visual Display Terminals, Taylor and Francis Ltd., London.

Linden, V. (1981) Er arbeid med dataskjermer helsefarlig? (Is working with VDUs dangerous to your health?) DATA, 1–2, 1981, (in Norwegian).

Smith, M. J., Stammerjohn, L. W., Cohen, B. G. F. and Lalich, N. R. (1980) Job stress in video display operations, in E. Grandjean and E. Vigliani (eds), Ergonomic Aspects of Visual Display Terminals, Taylor and Francis Ltd., London.

Smith, M. J., Cohen, B. G. F., Stammerjohn, L. W., and Happ, A. (1981) *An investigation of health complaints and job stress in video display operations,* NIOSH, U.S. Dept. of Health and Human Services, Cincinnati, Ohio 45226.

Thoresen, K. (ed.) (1978) *Terminalarbeidsplasser,* (Terminal work stations), Tanum-Norli, 1980 (in Norwegian).

Vifladt, (1980) Trygd – Data – Miljö (Social security – EDP – Work environment), Thesis for 'Social Security' (in Norwegian).

Wynn, E. (1979) Office Conversation as an Information Medium. Ph.D dissertation, Department of Anthropology, UCLA, Berkeley.

Description and modelling in EDP systems development

Petter Håndlykken

1 INTRODUCTION

To progressively larger groups of employees, the use of EDP systems have become part of their work, and for many of them, the design of these systems will largely determine the organizational framework they work in.

There is a growing understanding that designing and introducing EDP systems in a wider perspective, is closely related to designing and changing organizations. There has been a growing demand to make explicit the assumptions about the organization surrounding an EDP system, on which the design of a system is based (Newman, 1980). This implies demands for descriptions and models of the systems and of the environment in which the systems are intended to be used.

Design and change of organizations is strongly linked to key interests of management as well as employees. In Norway employees have a right to participate in these activities by virtue of the Working Environment Act and through technology agreements.

Employee participation in the design of the systems will often presuppose models that present a realistic picture of the consequences of the systems. Therefore it is important to discuss what such models comprise and for what purposes they may be used.

Methods for developing EDP systems are based on several types of model. This article attempts to summarize and discuss their use in systems development.

Firstly the article presents some fundamental concepts relating to description of EDP systems. Two different ways of describing an EDP system will be presented. The first describes an EDP system as an integrated part of the organization. The requirements to be met by the EDP system are drawn from models of the organization. These models are used in strategies for organizational change. The second describes the information contained in the EDP system. Requirements to be met by the EDP system are drawn from analysing the content of the information used by the organization and deriving 'conceptual models' of the EDP system.

The more complex systems become, the more important it is to make clear on what assumptions the systems are based. Better opportunities to experiment with systems during their development and phased introduction, do not reduce the importance of such models. Various techniques are being used for modelling and description. The experience with such techniques has, however, not always been advantageous. Designing techniques in this field will still be a topic for research within systems design.

In the last section, I will discuss techniques mentioned above, and one in particular: the DELTA language, which has been developed at the Norwegian Computing Centre. I will briefly present fundamental concepts of the language and refer to experiences from its use.

Initially, it may be useful to define a few concepts that occur in this article. A detailed discussion of the concepts can be found in Holbæk-Hanssen, Håndlykken and Nygaard, (1975).

By a *system* I mean a part of the world which a person or group, during a period of time, and for a distinct purpose, choose to regard as a whole. A system consists of parts: objects. To each object there may be associated properties and actions, and these may also involve other objects.

By a *model* I mean a system which in one way or another resembles another system: the reference system. The model is often used to imply properties of the reference system.

By a *description* I mean a written or oral presentation formulated in a language. Descriptions concerning a system will be termed 'system descriptions'.

2 TWO WAYS OF DESCRIBING AN EDP SYSTEM

Descriptions and models of electronic data processing systems are mainly used for the following three purposes:

— as a basis for communication and decision-making relating to the design of and changes in the data processing system and its environment;
— as a basis for the development and maintenance of computer programs and hardware;
— to convey information about the system to people who use or are going to use it. Such information may be necessary in order to understand the function of the system and data supplied by it.

During systems development, descriptions are made in a variety of ways. Some of them give a broad survey of the main features of the system. Others describe, in detail, how the system operates.

When we need to describe a data processing system, we may choose between two different approaches. According to information theory, the system is fully defined when all communication between the system and its environment is described. We can therefore define the system by stating the requirements for all input and output data and otherwise regard it as a 'black box' with unknown contents. This approach involves two main problems.

— It limits understanding of the content of the information processed by the system, which is an essential prerequisite of a data processing system.
— A description of the internal conceptual structure of an EDP system is highly desirable as a basis for programming the system, particularly if the system is to be altered and further developed at a later stage.

The problems with the approach became obvious when more comprehensive data banks (data bases) were built. It was therefore regarded as important to describe the conceptual structure of a data base by means of a 'conceptual model'. Principles for constructing such models have been one of the main topics of research on data bases for the last ten years. For less comprehensive systems, there has been an increasing use of descriptions of the concepts on which the system is based (Jackson, 1979). Thereby the content of the system will not be regarded as a 'black box', but as one or more *models*. The models define the concepts on which the system is based by giving a particular picture of some reality outside the system. Input data to and output data from the EDP system are regarded as communication between these models and the system environment.

In this paper I will assume that an EDP system is described by:

— *models* contained in the system;
— *communication* between the models contained in the system and the system environment.

Models contained in the system reflect the matters of fact which the system is to convey information about. An invoicing system of a firm for example, will be a model reflecting customer behaviour and deliveries of the firm. An accounting and budgeting system will contain a model of financial transactions and financial planning and control. An EDP system could normally be seen as containing several models, including one which represents the environment of the system (those who are communicating through it, the hardware it uses etc). The models contained in an EDP system are usually formalized in order to make use of standardized procedures for decision-making, statistics etc.

Communication between the models contained in the system and their environment includes the 'language' in which communication is expressed, and the equipment used for this communication. Communication can occur with people (for example via a visual display unit), and with other equipment (for example, other EDP systems). Communications can modify and update the contents of the EDP system (for example, updating a data base or including a new computer program).

An example may illustrate these concepts. Consider a planning department at a shipyard, where three clerks are employed: A, B and C. They use an EDP system (EDP) which supplies them with information about the present position of shipbuilding at the yard (see Fig. 1). The EDP system is to reproduce the building activity which takes place at the shipyard and therefore has to contain a model of the shipbuilding process.

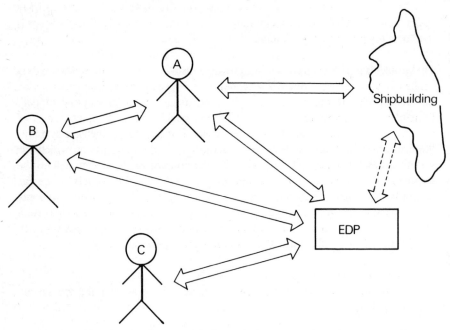

Fig. 1 – Planning department with three clerks A, B and C who use an EDP system when planning the building of ships.

A, B, and C will collect their information about the building activity partly from the EDP system, partly through contact with other people at the yard, and partly by observations of the building at the yard. This information along with A, B and C's knowledge of shipbuilding, are used as a basis for planning. Information from the EDP system is easy to interpret and to compare with information from other sources only if the model of shipbuilding contained in the system is in accordance with the conception of shipbuilding on which A, B and C otherwise base their work.

A, B and C wish to have information from the EDP system which supports the various tasks performed in the planning department. Communication between the clerks and the EDP system will have to be arranged according to the work organization in the planning department.

The requirement for models to be included in an EDP system, and the requirements for communication between the system and the environment are both necessary for systems design. In order to establish these requirements, various methods of analysis and description are used.

One such analysis puts the main emphasis on how the EDP system is to be used for solving tasks in its environment. Descriptions of work routines and prcesses, and their requirements, are used as a basis for systems design. This is frequently termed a function-oriented approach to design. In our example such a description would comprise tasks and work organization within the planning department of the shipyard.

Another type of analysis puts the main emphasis on analysing the content of the information used by the organization. The EDP system is described in terms of the models to be realized within it. This is often termed a 'data-oriented' approach to design. In our example such a description would comprise how shipbuilding is reproduced in the EDP system.

In practice, these two approaches will complement each other: both are important to the design of the system. Methods for developing EDP systems are however often called 'function-oriented' or 'data-oriented' according to which of these two types of descriptions are considered most significant in the method.

As a basis for systems design, we have to use descriptions of how the EDP system is applied in the user organization, as well as descriptions of its information content. Sections 3 and 4 explain these needs more fully.

3 THE ENVIRONMENT IN WHICH AN EDP SYSTEM IS USED

When designing an EDP system, it is necessary to make assumptions about the environment in which the system is to be used. Assumptions can be made implicitly during the design or they can be formulated explicitly as a model of the environment in which the system is intended to be used. The assumptions made can be complex even for a system which is limited to the performance of a single function within the organization, such as word processing (Newman, 1980).

Often the design of an EDP system will be closely related to the design of the organization surrounding it. Descriptions and models used for design of an EDP system, should therefore be related to those used for design of organizations. Models used for design of organizations may have several purposes:

— to assess analytically properties of an organization from certain objectives, for example to what extent it contributes to achievement of specified goals;
— to make the members of the organization support a particular view of the organization and its environment (organizational ideology);

— as a basis for communication within the organization; for training and for the exchange of ideas, knowledge and experience;
— to act as agreements between interested parties on future organization;
— to analyse specific consequences of alternative designs of EDP systems.

For design of organizations various techniques for description and modelling are used:

— models of formal organization; the distribution of benefits, responsibility and authority within the organiztion;
— socio-technical models of production input/output;
— models of work tasks and work procedures, job descriptions;
— models of financial control (budget and accounting models);
— models of decisions and rules for decision-making in the organization;
— models of the flow of information/data in the organization.

With regard to technical systems there is normally a substantial theoretical and empirical foundation which makes it possible to devise models which can predict properties of a system with high reliability. When it comes to social systems, such models do not exist, particularly if we want to explore a wide spectrum of properties of the system. The theory of organizations is not that far developed and existing empirical knowledge cannot be generalized in the same straightforward manner as for technical systems.

It is difficult to enforce one particular model as the basis for communication within an organization. The members of an organization will always have preconceived ideas of the organization and how it operates. The concepts are formed and chosen according to a perception of what is fundamental to the organization. Some factors are stressed at the expense of others. It is often presented as a question of 'presenting the right thing in the proper context'.

Interest groups within an organization (for example, the management or a trade union) may use different concepts in their descriptions of the organization. The concepts could be connected with the need to look after specific interests. As a consequence they will focus attention on concepts important to these interests. So the choice of concepts and models may be linked to the question of interests. To elicit experience and knowledge from the lower ranks of the organization, it is important to use concepts related to the production process, working methods and the organization of work.

When designing EDP systems, one tends to put the main emphasis on defining the information requirements of the organization and to use techniques and models for defining these. This is based on the assumption that the essential function of an EDP system is to supply information according to predefined needs within the organization. However, if the EDP system is seen as a collection of tools available to the members of the organization this assumption may not be valid. The organization and methods of work may be even more important for the design of the tool than the 'information requirements.'

Although there are limitations to the conclusions that can be drawn from the use of analytic models, the use of such models are a prerequisite for analytic design. The models are necessary to make design choices and to explain on what premises the design of an EDP system is based. The requirements placed on models, will, however, depend on how they are used in the design process. We will therefore now discuss the design process and different 'strategies' for organizational design and change.

3.1 Strategies for organizational change

A change in organization is often preceeded by a process of analysis where models of the present as well as the future organization are developed. Based on these models a process of change is started where actual changes in organization structure are made. The two processes are illustrated in Fig. 2.

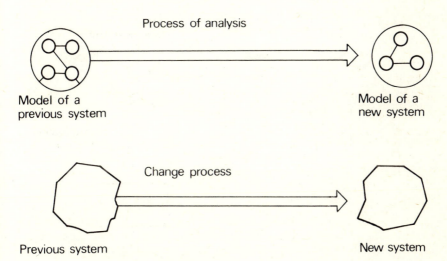

Fig. 2 – Process of analysis and change process.

The process of analysis implies that members of the organization, or the outside consultants, design models that reflect certain aspects of the organization's way of operating. The change process includes training, recruiting/dismissal of personnel, installation of equipment, altering of jobs and tasks etc. The specification and construction of an EDP system usually takes place after a model of the new organization has been drawn up. The substantial part of the EDP system has to be constructed before the actual change.

By looking at the relation between the two processes above, we can describe alternative strategies for the use of models for change in organizations. (φsterlund, 1974). The strategies can be termed:

- the 'never completed' strategy;
- the 'expert' strategy;
- the 'education' strategy;
- the 'process' strategy;
- the 'laboratory' strategy.

The 'never completed' strategy never goes beyond the analytical level. A model is worked out and shelved without being implemented. This is in fact no strategy for organizational change. (It may be a strategy for *not* changing the organization – 'the question is being investigated').

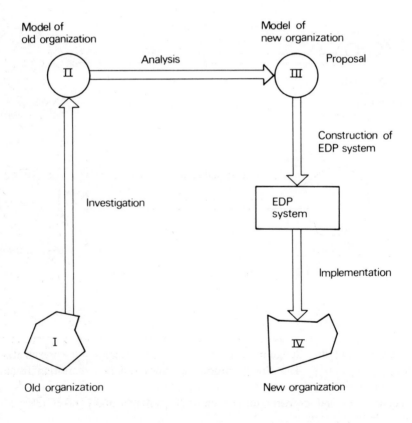

Fig. 3 – The 'expert strategy' for organizational change.

The *'expert strategy'* implies that a group (often outside the organization considered) formulate a new organizational model. Based on this, an EDP system is designed, which is used to realize the new organization. The organization passes from the old to the new form at a particular moment of time. The strategy is sketched out in Fig. 3.

In principle, the *education strategy* is similar to the expert strategy, but a main emphasis is put on a gradual organizational change from the old to the new model. The transition period allows for training and for members of the organization to gradually familiarize themselves with their tasks in the new organization. However, the final organization is already determined and the EDP system has been specified but not necessarily fully implemented before the changes start (see Fig. 4).

The *process strategy* differs from the previous strategies in that forming analytic models, construction and modification of the EDP system and changes in

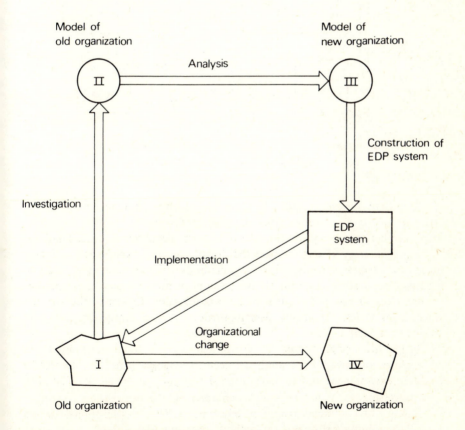

Fig. 4 – The 'education strategy' for organizational change.

the organization take place at the same time (see Fig. 5). The process is experimental in the way that the final result is not determined in advance. One presupposes that the goal can be altered during the change process without involving too many disruptions. The models are used for supporting experiments in cooperation with the members of the organization.

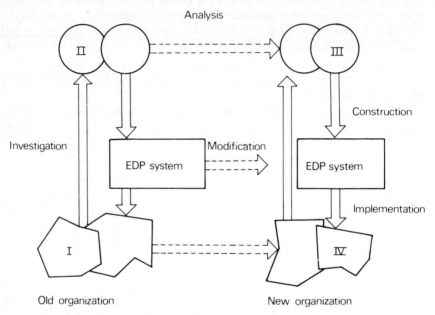

Fig. 5 — The 'process strategy' for organizational change.

The EDP system is gradually constructed and modified preferably by members of the organization itself. Outside experts have as their main task to teach members of the organization how to solve problems, not to realize solutions.

The *laboratory strategy* implies that the organization experiments with new organizational arrangements and working methods with minimum use of analytic models. The strategy may not always be implemented, because most changes require a certain amount of planning and coordination. Closest to this strategy are changes which are mainly person-oriented, such as group dynamics and sensitivity training.

In real life a single strategy of change will rarely be found in its pure form. An organization always has a continual need for changes in order to adjust to a changing environment and to solve internal problems. After an administrative data processing system has been implemented, it will still be necessary to modify the system with continual changes and adjustments. These organizational changes take place according to a 'process method' where the EDP system sets a limit to the changes that are possible to implement, without devising a completely new system. Necessary changes at this stage are called 'maintenance work'. It is a familiar problem that this work is often more extensive than the original development work, even for systems which are used for five years or less (Boehm, 1979).

3.2 Discussion of strategies in the development of EDP systems

Organizational changes in the administrative sector have traditionally occurred through gradual changes, according to a 'process method'. Learning by trial and error from gradual changes has been an important source of knowledge. The organizations have 'evolved' rather than been 'designed'.

In the development and introduction of administrative data processing systems, other methods have been used. This may be a deliberate choice of strategy, but may also be rooted in the fact that the systems have involved extensive organizational changes which are difficult to carry through gradual evolution. Moreover, the extent of the development of the EDP system and preparations in the form of equipment installation and data recording etc., have required working methods different from those used previously.

To solve these problems, attempts have been made at adjusting the methods which engineers use for building complex technical installations to include the development of information systems. This has not been very successful. One reason for this, is the problem of designing reliable models of organizations. The design and change of organizations require participation and use of extensive knowledge from the people involved. This makes the design process different from the corresponding process for technical systems.

The strategies for organizational change presented in the previous section can be discussed in relation to a number of aspects of system development. I will mention three such aspects.

— what practical consequences do the strategies have for the development of EDP systems? What resources are required to carry them into effect?
— what possibility do they provide for employee participation, insight and control in systems design?
— what qualities of the organization do they promote?

Most of the specification and development of EDP systems has traditionally been left to EDP experts outside the user departments. However, new technology and user-oriented programming languages now provide better possibilities of leaving all or some of the development work to 'non-programmers'. Less technical knowledge and considerably less work effort is required to write simple computer programs. This implies that programs can be developed and tried out before deciding whether they are going to be used ('experimental systems design'). Nevertheless, a 'process strategy' will normally require more resources, especially for training, and will be more time-consuming than the other strategies (Martin, 1981).

At the same time, a 'process strategy' will build up resources in the organization in the form of knowledge and capability of problem-solving and of further development. The strategies of change are then not equally valuable as regards the knowledge and potential for further changes they build up in the organization.

The Norwegian Work Environment Act has provisions concerning employee participation in organization changes. The 'process strategy' presupposes an accumulation of knowledge and a local level of activity which are completely in line with the intentions of the Act.

The degree of employee co-determination in a 'process strategy' will depend on the limits and the resources provided by the management. Strict control of detail and meagre resources may make it impossible to complete this process of change.

In the Norwegian agreement on employee participation in the public sector, negotiation between the management and the labour unions is used as a principle for employee participation. When negotiating, a clear distinction between the planning and the realization of changes may be an advantage. This is most easily obtained through the 'expert' and 'education' strategies. A particular model of a future organization can serve as the basis for negotiation and possibly as the basis of an agreement.

In some cases the management or the trade union will best look after their interests by negotiating a detailed agreement on the future organization before the change takes place. The model of the organization will establish a contract concerning the final goal of the change. It may, however, be difficult to know in advance the consequences of realizing a particular model. An agreement with unknown consequences is, however, not as valuable to the parties involved.

One single strategy of change will generally not be the best for every situation and from every point of view (Ehn and Sandberg, 1979, p. 137). The choice of strategy may be a question of interests.

The requirements demanded of descriptions and models used during the change, will depend on which strategy is used. An 'expert' or an 'education' strategy will emphasize models which make it possible to predict the consequences of organizational changes. As mentioned earlier such models generally do not exist. 'Unpredicted consequences' are often due to faulty models, and lack of thorough investigations.

With a 'process' strategy for organizational change it becomes less important to predict detailed consequences from models. Knowledge is to a greater extent obtained from practical experiments during the process. There will, however, be an increased emphasis on models which can be used by the members of the organization after a relatively short period of training.

All strategies emphasize the use of descriptions and models which are easily 'communicable'. This implies descriptions based on concepts which are already known in the organization. New concepts should be related to those used before. The communicability will also depend on the form of presentation.

However, the set of concepts seems to be more important than the form of presentation. So new methods for presentation will hardly be enough to ensure progress in this field.

Some methods for the development of systems presuppose a division into phases of work where every phase is based on a specific type of model. The kinds of models thus decides the order in which problems will be dealt with. The order could be decisive for the result of the process of change. Previous decisions establish a pattern for latter decisions. Postponing a decision to a later stage, may in fact be a way of disguising a particular decision (Perrow, 1974). Models intended to be used in development work divided into such phases, may be difficult to adjust to a 'process' strategy.

It has been argued that 'process' strategies and the gradual introduction of new systems, in the future will lead to less demand for analytic models during systems development. If we assume that organizations will be changed by evolution rather than conscious design, this may be true. This, however, does not seem likely. Learning from experiments will also be much more effective when supported by an analytic approach.

4 THE INFORMATION CONTAINED IN AN EDP SYSTEM

In the previous section we discussed the use of descriptions and models of the environment in which an EDP system is used. Within the environment it often seems natural to describe the EDP system by the functions or tasks which it is able to perform. The development work will also require descriptions which focus on the meaning of the information processed by and contained in the EDP system. The purposes of such descriptions are:

- to enable the users of the system to understand how it operates and to understand data from the system;
- to form the basis of programming the EDP system, as a necessary supplement to the description of the functions the system is to perform.

As a consequence, the requirement on these types of descriptions will differ considerably from requirements on descriptions mentioned in the previous section.

The flow of information within an organization in general assumes certain models or 'classification forms' which reflect the reaility in which the organization is working. An organization has often developed its own set of concepts or its own jargon for internal communication. Everything which is in accordance with this set of concepts can be efficiently communicated within the organization. The set of concepts forms a basis for deciding what matters are to be further reported to other persons and other departments in the organization. It may be directly or indirectly described in a formalized information system, or it may merely be a tradition in the organization.

The set of concepts is in general based on professional knowledge related to the production. It will however also reflect the predominant aims and interests in the organization. The understanding of a production process is not a purely technical question. This can be illustrated from our example in Section 2: what attention should the planning of production at the shipyard pay to not moving heavy objects over the deck of a ship while painting is done in the hull (because of the noise nuisance?) The question cannot be answered as a technical matter only.

Matters which are described by means of the set of concepts used in the organization will be far easier to communicate than matters not described in accordance with the set of concepts. The ability to define and influence the set of concepts which the organization uses about itself, is an important instrument for management and control in an organization (Perrow, 1974).

An EDP system will only be a part of the information system within an organization. The system is supplemented by other formal and informal ways of exchanging information. The concepts used in the EDP system will have an influence on the set of concepts used in other information systems.

If the EDP system is to become an integrated part of the information system of the organization, the concepts used have to agree with concepts in other systems used in the organization. There are two extreme ways of obtaining such integration:

— by formulating the concepts of the EDP system to closely agree with the set of concepts already used in the organization;
— by changing the set of concepts used in the organization so that it corresponds with the concepts in the EDP system.

The first procedure may be the easiest to follow by designing an EDP system based on the former system in the organization (manual or mechanical). Normally, however, this assumes that the system only involves minor alterations in existing routines. This may be illustrated by the example from Section 2. The staff in the planning department have, through training and experience, formed their own concept of shipbuilding. When A interprets data from the EDP system, she will relate these to her own understanding of the building process and her own concept of how the EDP system reproduces it. To make data from the EDP system easy to interpret for A, the concepts about shipbuilding used in the system ought to be close to the concepts normally used by A about shipbuilding.

An investigation into five fully developed systems in Sweden, reveals that EDP systems 'copying' previous manual systems have been less problematic to introduce than the systems not doing that (Docherty et al., 1977). This could indicate that many of the problems arising during the introduction of EDP systems, cannot be attributed to equipment, but rather to the new set of concepts introduced through the systems or to other changes introduced by the systems.

The problems attached to changing the concepts used in an organization, and the need for training it requires, may be substantial. However, an EDP system often requires a change of concepts. A change in production technology through *automation* may require this. A new system often assumes *integration* of the information systems in different parts of the organization. In order to obtain this, it may be necessary to change the concepts.

This may also be illustrated by the example from Section 2. It might be that A and B each perform one part of the planning task, and therefore use different concepts of the building process. If both of them are to collect data from the same EDP system, this system must be based on a conception of the building process which is common to A and B. This could make it necessary to change former concepts.

When developing an EDP system, forming the concepts on which the system is to be based, is considered one of the most difficult activities. The concepts used within a system, and within different systems, should be consistent and unambiguous. However there also has to be possibilities for changing and introducing new concepts.

EDP technology generally leads to an increased emphasis on the definition of concepts in terms of measurable properties and formal rules for decision-making. The concepts used in the EDP system therefore have to be specified in a different and more precise way than definitions of concepts in natural language.

A common philosophy for defining models to be incorporated in an EDP system is that there should be a 'one to one' relationship between what are experienced as objects in the modelled environment and objects in the model. This approach implies that objects in models should be equipped with the same properties and behaviour as are ascribed to objects in the environment. What are experienced as natural objects in the modelled environment will certainly depend on the area of subject in which the system is used and the tasks carried out by it.

The functions an EDP system is supposed to perform will decide which models has to be contained in it. At the same time the models will be a basis for defining the functions of the system. During systems development, there will be an interplay between specifying the functions of the EDP system and designing models showing its contents.

Often main features of the models within an EDP system, remain largely unchanged whereas the functions will frequently be subject to alterations. The reason for this is that the concepts within the subject area in question are relatively permanent. By designing software for an EDP system on the basis of the models, the basic structure of the software will not be altered, despite new demands on the system. This simplifies maintenance and further development of the EDP system considerably.

In recent years, more attention has been paid to the use of models of information content in the development of EDP systems (various 'data modelling'-methods 'Jackson Structured Design' etc.). A series of techniques and 'languages' have been developed for the purpose. The DELTA language, which will be dealt with in the next section, is also a technique for such modelling.

5 TECHNIQUES FOR DESCRIPTION AND MODELLING. THE DELTA LANGUAGE

Description and modelling in the development of EDP systems may be performed without particular techniques or aids. However, considerable advantages are obtained when using specific techniques.

— It is necessary to have precise descriptions as a basis of systems design. This may
   be very difficult to obtain by using natural language and 'ad hoc' conventions.
— By using uniform and well-defined concepts, techniques can improve the
   consistency and overview, and make it easier to deduct consequences from a
   proposed design.
— When those who participate in development work use common techniques,
   it may become easier for each participant to understand what the others
   are doing.

The main problem seems to be that there is no well developed theory of system development on which the techniques may be based. A series of linguistic techniques have, however, been devised. These are generally based on a specific set of fundamental concepts with a defined meaning. Moreover, there are rules for the definition of new concepts based on these fundamental concepts, which ensure that the new concepts are given a precise meaning. The techniques in general include rules defining the syntax of a description and drawing graphic illustrations etc.

The use of techniques of this kind may lead to serious problems. Some of the typical problems are:

— Fundamental concepts are aimed at describing certain conception of reality,
   whereas other conceptions of the same reality cannot be expressed. For
   example, with a method of description which is aimed at describing data and
   the flow of data in an organization, it would be difficult to describe other
   aspects such as the organization of work. This implies that alternative description have to be made, in order to show other aspects.
— Logically simple fundamental concepts in a language, often lead to comprehensive and over-complex descriptions of relatively trivial matters. This is so
   because 'everyday and easily understandable' matters logically may be very
   complex.

— Fundamental concepts that are logically more complex, generally assume a classification of the objects in a system into a few basic categories like 'activities', 'resources', 'processes', 'objects' and 'relations'. Thereby the user of the language is forced to make a fundamental classification of objects according to these concepts. The classification will not always make it possible to define concepts which are natural and useful in a specific situation.

— Use of these techniques may require extensive training and they may be difficult to comprehend for those without EDP education.

During the years 1973–75, the Norwegian Computing Centre carried through a research project where a set of concepts and a language (known as the DELTA language) for system description were developed. The background for developing the language was the need for techniques for description and modelling in the development of EDP systems. The starting point for the project was the programming language SIMULA (developed at the Norwegian Computing Centre). The concepts in SIMULA had in many ways proved to be appropriate for describing complex systems. However, SIMULA has limitations as a general language for system description, since it is a programming language for digital computers. The DELTA language is not a programming language and is then not restricted by such limitations.

The DELTA language is a formal language and a precise way of interpreting descriptions in the language has therefore been established. The intention is, however, that concepts of the language also may be used when composing descriptions in natural language. The DELTA language has been defined in a comprehensive report (in English) (Holbæk-Hanssen, Håndlykken and Nygaard, 1975). There is a shorter Norwegian introduction to the language (Holbæk-Hanssen, 1978) and a short presentation of the language (in English) (Håndlykken and Nygaard, 1980).

The DELTA language is used to describe *systems*. In the language a system is described in the following way.

A *system* is a part of the world which a person or a group, during a period of time and for a distinct purpose, choose to regard as a whole. A system consists of parts: objects. To each object there may be associated properties and actions, and these may also involve other objects.

The objects of a system described in the DELTA language are hierarchically arranged. There is one object, the system object, which represents the system as a whole. The system object *contains* objects which may again contain associated objects etc.

According to the definition, properties and actions can be attached to objects:

— *quantities* which indicate properties which can be measured according to a scale of values;

— *references* indicating the object's knowledge of other objects in the system;
— *patterns* describing possible rules of action, possible internal objects or possible types of properties associated with the object.

An object may also have an associated sequence of actions which the object performs within the period of time in which it exists. The actions are defined by indicating, in order of succession, individual actions performed by the object. Each individual action may affect properties of the object itself and other objects in the system, and may take a period of time to perform. All objects in a system may perform actions simultaneously. One object may interrupt an action executed by another object by sending an interrupt request to the object.

Often a system contains a set of objects which have similar properties and which can perform the same kinds of actions. In the DELTA language such objects constitute a *class* of objects. A class of objects is described by one common description. If a system contains a number of persons, these objects may be described by *one* description which says that each of these has properties like name, address, date of birth etc. The actual values of these properties will however be different for the different persons.

Within a class of objects, we may identify subsets of objects which differ from the others by having common properties in addition to the properties of other objects in the class. Such subsets are termed *subclasses* of objects. For example, persons with a particular occupation may be described as a subclass of persons, with specific properties in addition to those of persons in general.

In the development of EDP systems, the DELTA language may be applied in several ways. One way is to use the fundamental concepts only. Setting the boundary for a system, identifying named objects and classes of objects, identifying and naming the properties of these objects. This may be done without using any particular description syntax. Such use of the language could for example be suitable for organizational descriptions.

A precise description of properties of objects in a system will often be needed. We may want an accurate description of the value range of quantities and the rules for calculating a specific value. The DELTA language has a formally defined syntax similar to a programming language, which may be used for such purposes. The formal syntax will be suitable for describing EDP systems and in connection with some types of analyses.

The DELTA language has been used in the development of a large administrative data processing system. Experience indicates that the linguistic concepts are useful for designing 'procedure-oriented' descriptions of an organization. The fundamental concepts of the language describing actions are suitable in this connection (identifying and naming rules of action and describing interrupts). Procedure-oriented descriptions of organizations in other connections also seem useful in the development of EDP systems (Newman, 1980).

The language has been useful for defining models of information contained in an EDP system. The particularly strong aspect of the language is its concepts for description of time and actions. These are normally weak points of other aids of this kind.

The language seems to allow the inclusion of several disimilar aspects of a system in the one description. Since the language only has one powerful fundamental concept (the object), the objects of a system do not have to belong to predefined categories.

The language requires considerable training to be used effectively. There is little educational material available today suitable for systems design.

The DELTA language has not been introduced as a product for common use in systems design. The DELTA project primarily aimed at contributing to research relating to aids for system description, and must be evaluated accordingly. The language has evoked interest in a series of research environments and has been an inspiration to researchers in their further work, particularly at the University of Århus in Denmark and at the Norwegian Computing Centre.

At the international level, there is currently much activity in the area of developing techniques for administrative systems design. The techniques are based on assumptions about systems design and organizational change which are not always made explicit. A common feature seems to be that none of them are based on an extensive theory of systems design. The development of such a theory seems necessary both to be able to develop new methods and techniques and to evaluate what is offered today.

REFERENCES

Boehm, B. W. (1979) Software Engineering: R & D trends and Defence Needs, in *Research Directions in Software Technology*, edited by P. Wegner, The MIT Press, Cambridge, Mass.

Docherty, P., et al. (1977) *Hur man lyckas med system utveckling – en analys av fem praktikfall* (How to succeed with systems development – an analysis of five cases), EFI, Handelshøgskolan i Stockholm, Stockholm, 1977 (in Swedish).

Ehn, P., and Sandberg, Å. (1979) Företagsstyring och løntagarmakt (Enterprise management and employee's power), Arbetslivscentrum, Stockholm (in Norwegian).

Holbæk-Hanssen, E., Håndlykken, P., and Nygaard, K. (1975) *System Description and the DELTA Language*, Norwegian Computing Centre, Oslo.

Holbæk-Hanseen, E. (1978), *En kort innføring i DELTA-språket og DELTA-strukturerte systemer* (An introduction to the DELTA language and DELTA-structured systems), publ. nr. 599, Norsk Regnesentral, Oslo (in Norwegian).

Håndlykken, P., and Nygaard, K. (1980) The DELTA system description language – Motivation, main concepts and experiences from use, in *Software Engineering Environments* edited by H. Hunke, North-Holland, Amsterdam.

Jackson, M. A. (1979) Information systems: modelling, sequencing and transformations, *Proceedings of the 3rd International Conference on Software Engineering, IEEE, 1978.*

Martin, J. (1981) *Application Development without Programmers,* Savant Institute, Carnforth, Lancashire.

Newman, W. (1980) Office models and office systems design, in *Integrated Office Systems – Burotics,* Naffah (ed.), North-Holland, Amsterdam.

Perrow, C. (1974) *Organisasjonsteori – en kritisk analyse* (Organizational theory – a critical analysis), Fremad, København (in Danish).

Østerlund, J. E. (1974) Førendringsprocessor och organisationsutveckling, from *Organisationsutveckling* (Process of change and organizational development, from Organization Development), Lennart Rolin (ed.), Gleerups OU-serie, Lund (in Swedish).

The office of the future–some sociological perspectives on office work and office technology

Arne Pape

1 INTRODUCTION

According to a series of studies which have been presented during the last years, we are facing dramatic changes in working conditions and employment in the office sector. Siemens is said to have estimated that it will be possible to automate functions equating to 40 percent of all office jobs in West Germany by 1990. Nora and Minc (1978) predict a 30 percent reduction of employment in insurance and banking in France by 1990. In Great Britain, there are estimates indicating a reduction of 600 000 office jobs by 1983, which corresponds to 15 percent of the general office workers (APEX, 1979). Other investigations have presented similar findings. By 1990 the demand for office workers will be reduced by some 30 percent and an unemployment rate of 15–20 percent has been predicted for office workers during the next 15 years (See Bird 1980).

Such predictions have, for obvious reasons, evoked lively discussion about the developments in the office sector. From many quarters, measures are being demanded to ensure a controlled use of new office technology, in accordance with generally accepted objectives concerning employment and working conditions. However, it is not quite clear what is meant by control in this connection and to what extent and in what way technological development in the office sector can be controlled. If 'control' involves a systematic use of measures with tried and tested results this cannot, as yet, be applied to office technology. None the less this development is subject to social, economic and political pressures which will cause considerable changes compared to what is considered to be technically feasible and financially profitable today.

On this important issue many people will criticize the prognoses or studies of the future presented in the past few years. Such predictions seem to contradict the general experience of technological development in the office sector. The late 1970s is not the first time dramatic forecasts have been made using existing technology to illustrate changes in employment and working conditions in the office sector. Both in the 1930s and in the 1950s, similar studies of the future were presented. Mills (1951), Lockwood (1958), and Braverman (1974) give references to earlier discussions about the future office. As a rule, prognoses based on technological possibilities have not been correct. Despite technical and organizational innovations which one believed would involve dramatic changes, the development in the office sector has largely shown the same trends observed over the last hundred years:

— Employment in the office sector has increased both in total numbers and in percentage of the employed population.
— Increasing numbers of office employees are women.
— Differences in salaries and wages between office employees and workers in the manufacturing industries are decreasing.
— The increase in productivity in office work is low as compared with other sectors of the economy.

Despite a series of innovations such as EDP, copying machines and open-plan offices, the last twenty years have largely continued along traditional lines. From 1972 to 1979 the number of office employees in Norway increased by 32 percent, i.e. from 13.6 to 15.9 percent of the employed population. The percentage of women working in offices increased from 50.6 to 54.9 percent. From 1973 to 1979, the average salary for white-collar employees in the manufacturing industries increased by 88.6 percent, whereas the average wage increase for industrial workers was 90.2 percent. Although it is difficult to measure productivity in office work, there seems to be general agreement that the growth rate has been low for the last 20 years. In the USA, statistical estimates of productivity during the period from 1968 to 1978 indicate a 4 percent increase for office workers, as opposed to 83 percent among industrial workers (Haider, 1979).

We are even less certain of the changes that have taken place in the organization of office work. Official statistics provide little information of that kind. One view of office systems claims that the introduction of EDP has involved considerable changes which lead towards factory-like organization in offices. However, research on organizational impacts of the use of EDP gives little evidence that the introduction of EDP has resulted in far-reaching and unambiguous changes in office organization (Kling, 1980). Both foreign investigations of office work (Newmann, 1979; Wynn, 1979) and Norwegian investigations of the working environment in offices (Norsk Produktivitetsinstitutt, 1981), give reason to believe that the impact of EDP on the organization of office work has not been as extensive as people tend to believe. But the impact has certainly been serious enough for those who are directly affected.

How can technical development be defined in relation to the general development in office work and management? What are the future prospects viewed in the light of experience of current technical development in office work? These questions will be discussed in this article. The discussion divides into two parts.

Firstly a presentation of different aspects of office work and office technology will be discussed from a sociological perspective. The office will be considered here as a separate part of an organization, with functions related to information and management which are separate from the general production task of the organization. These functions are determined by the relation between organizations and institutional conditions in their environment. To discuss the relation between the use of data technology, functional demands on office work and structural aspects of the work organization. Finally, we will discuss the various explanations for why the use of data technology in office work does not have the consequences that are expected. The following three assertions will be commented on:

- Offices are constantly taking in new functions and tasks.
- The organization of office work complicates the process of mechanization to a greater extent than people have realized.
- The resistance to changes has been stronger and more effective than expected.

Secondly the article deals with the design of new office techniques and new methods of organizing office work. This will be looked at in terms of the production of new knowledge. The central issue here is how the development of basic technology − particularly micro-electronics − will influence the way this production of knowledge is organized. It is partly a question of the product strategies of the equipment and systems manufacturers, but it is also a question of adjustment and development strategies of the offices that will make use of the new technology.

2 SOME STRUCTURAL FEATURES OF OFFICE WORK

2.1 Growth in office tasks − production technology and institutional changes

The increase in white-collar employees as a percentage of the employed population, can be attributed at two different economic trends (Elliot, 1977). First of all, there has been a shift in employment to sectors, industries and types of business where office workers represent a large proportion of total employees. Typical examples are the developments in the public sector, banking, insurance, and the wholesale trade. Another factor is a shift in various types of business where technical and organizational changes have resulted in a relative increase in office employees as compared with other groups of personnel. This applies particularly to the manufacturing industries. In 1950, salaried staff represented 15 percent of the employees in the Norwegian manufacturing industries, as opposed to 22 percent in 1974. It is primarily the latter trend we have in mind when referring to the general growth in office tasks, or the fact that office work becomes an increasingly dominant part of various types of business. From an organizational point of view, we must distinguish between changes in office tasks which arise from internal factors in the enterprise or organization and those which are associated with external factors such as changes in the market structure or the institutional framework of the organization.

Internal changes are largely related to technical and organizational changes undertaken to achieve the aims of production, i.e. changes in production technology. A central hypothesis concerning the developments in production technology, implies that change has been associated with a redistribution of knowledge which in turn has established a dividing line between physical production and the management and control of production. Management and control functions have been taken over by groups, other than production workers, resulting in an overall growth in tasks for salaried staff and office employees.

Technical knowledge in an organization has been transferred from production to management. Such competence, vital for the production activity, now lies with technical and professional staff who are organizationally placed as part of the administrative machinery of the enterprise. Moreover, quantitative enlargement of office tasks has led to a professionalization of control and management of production (Braverman, 1974).

The relation between changes in administrative tasks and changes in the institutional framework of organizations is a complex social process. Organizational growth and a stronger interaction of bureaucracies, professional and industrial bodies, and markets, tend to result in increasing demands on the administrative machinery of organizations. People claim that organizations are becoming increasingly complex, which puts new and greater demands on control and management (Simon, 1976; Newman and Ward, 1980).

Other social therotists take the opposite view and have interpreted institutional changes as resulting from the organizations' strategies towards their environment. Williamson (1975) maintains that changes in institutional conditions are often a result of attempts at economizing within a limited capacity to make rational decisions, thus reducing the costs of transactions with the environment.

If we follow this theory, the growth in office work and management is paradoxical. How can attempts at reducing costs of control and management result in institutional changes which increase the demands on information handling and on management? An example of how this may occur and the role of technology in such an institutional transformation in the Norwegian wholesale market is included below.

Over the past 20 years, the Norwegian wholesale market for everyday commodities has been subject to far-reaching structural changes. During this period, the wholesale trade was commissioned to form amalgamations, which through cooperation with retailers established four large integrated units. These cooperative agreements were developed through systematizing and improving the efficiency of contacts between wholesale firms and retailers. The principle is that every retailer has one wholesale firm as his main supplier. They agree upon regular purchasing routines. The wholesale firm receives orders at fixed times, and the flow of information is accelerated through standardization and formalization. The system is based on agreements on prices and discounts which reward steady customers who conform to agreed procedures.

By these agreements, profits are tied to a simplification and standardization of routines connected with the ordering and delivery of goods. When the agreement has been concluded, the actual sales are conducted according to fixed administrative routines.

The employment of data technology has in several ways played an active role in this development. When it comes to the purchasing routines standardization and formalization of information have given rise to extensive use of computer-based systems. One example is the use of portable terminals. Such routines are usually based on particular ways of arranging and marking the shelves in a shop, which makes it easy to discover whether it is time to re-order stock. The ordering is done by keying stock data into a small and inexpensive data recording unit, the size of a pocket calculator. This unit can be coupled to the telephone network to be read into a computer. In this way routines are established that involve considerable administrative rationalization and better control of the daily business for both parties (Pape 1981).

The problem is that competition between the parties is disturbed. When agreements have been entered into a change of partners will involve considerable costs, with the retailer suffering most. It is the wholesale firms, however, who design and offer cooperative agreements and therefore it is the retailer who must rearrange his systems accordingly. A difference in access to information will occur, for example because the wholesale firm has easy access to information about the retailer's activity, whereas the retailer does not obtain corresponding information about the wholesale firm. Owing to the complexity of the agreements, the retailers have difficulty in comparing them in terms of their benefits. Moreover, there is a strong concentration of power in the wholesale business, where four amalgamations control more than 95 percent of the market.

Consequently, the retailer's bargaining strength is reduced and the total gains of rationalization become unevenly distributed, to the advantage of the wholesale firm. This represents a political problem. Such a tendency contributes to a wider gap between what is profitable and the public benefit, and may bring about political control measures from the authorities. Such measures will entail higher costs of transactions, which at least on a national scale, may lead to an increase in administrative tasks.

Corresponding trends are to be found in other commercial activities. We can assume that in other industries, similar information systems can be used for integration and cooperation between different enterprises. The employment of technology in the commodity trade is not unique. In several important areas, the use of such technology has been connected with institutional changes. The introduction of salary payments into bank accounts made it possible to rationalize the methods of payment in banks, as well as the pay systems of the enterprises. By means of regulations that can be automatically effected, the relationship between the public and the administration would change, to open possibilities for a thorough rationalization of public adminsitration.

Technology can enable us to find rational models of cooperation, both by making it possible to administer extremely complex agreements and by making it possible to devise organizational agreements that involve financial gains for all parties. In administration and office work, this development could have the following results:

− Simplified transactions between sectors could reduce the costs of information.
− Cooperative agreements could give rise to a more rational organization of administration across the borderlines of the enterprises.
− Counter-moves from the authorities or from trade rivals could require increased administrative effort.
− From traditional adjustment to the market, activities could be directed towards negotiations between enterprises and various authorities. Aministrative tasks in connection with the political functions of the enterprises could increase.

In society as a whole, administrative technology could become a decisive factor as to how interaction will be organized in an institutionalized framework. In particular, the question of which transactions will be organized through markets and which will be organized within organizations, depends on what information technology is available.

We have seen that the development in the office sector is tied to changes in production technology and institutional conditions. However, there will always be large variations between different kinds of business, and office tasks and work patterns in different organizations will reflect this. The nature of the tasks and the organization will be extremely diverse in schools, trade unions and industrial concerns. The size of the offices is an indication of this. In 1976, 42 percent of the Norwegian industrial concerns had a salaried staff of less than ten employees, whereas 50 percent of the salaried staff were employed in enterprises with more than one hundred salaried staff members (Likestillingsrådet, 1977).

When it comes to technical changes in the office sector, there are two features which may be explained by such differences. Firstly, different demands for efficiency will be made by different offices, both regarding how the demands occur and what sort of efficiency is demanded. There are, for example, different demands made on private enterprise and the public sector. The importance of office productivity will depend on how important office labour costs are in relation to other costs. Secondly, different tasks result in varying organizational structures, which implies that technical change will be carried through in dissimilar ways. Consequently, there are few indications that the office sector is going to adjust to new office technology in a clear-cut and simple way.

2.2 Office organization — labour market and the structure of qualifications

On the basis of an analysis of the traditional office, Lockwood (1958) has described how structural aspects of the office worker's occupational knowledge are tied to the organization of office work. According to Lockwood, the two important aspects are the labour market structure in the office sector and the use of knowledge in the execution of practical office work.

Like craftsmen, the traditional clerk acquired his knowledge through practical experience. But contrary to the craftsman's case, the relevance of this knowledge would often be restricted to the particular enterprise. This made the clerk's qualifications difficult to 'sell' in the open labour market. They were either of too little value to other firms, or their value consisted of the business secrets of a trade rival. As a result, there was a considerable discrepancy between the value of a clerk's knowledge to a certain firm and the value of his qualifications in the open market. He could be practically indispensable to his firm, whereas his general competence was not in particular demand in the labour market. His future prospects depended on his ability to acquire the qualifications specific to the firm, and the possibilities to 'sell' his qualifications in order to obtain promotions. A clerk's career and interests have always been tied to the internal labour market.

The concept 'internal labour market' is taken from labour market theory and has been defined as 'an administrative unit where the price and distribution of labour are determined by a set of administrative rules, and not by supply and demand in a market' (Doeringer and Piore, 1971). We want to use the concept to describe a work organization where such a market function is particularly predominant and where the demands for qualifications — normative as well as technical — are marked by this.

Apart from being specific to one enterprise, a clerk's qualifications were difficult to assess. As opposed to the work of salesmen and industrial workers, the value of the work of a clerk is difficult to measure in terms of financial output. Traditionally there were few prescribed rules or established routines for the assessment and evaluation of a clerk's qualifications. From a general impression of the clerk and a vague notion of his usefulness to the firm, the management was to decide what qualifications were relevant and valuable, whether the particular clerk possessed such qualifications and how to reward him.

Conditions relating to qualifications and labour markets can be associated with certain characteristics of office environments. There is, for example, the relatively high degree of loyalty to the firm together with competition and the importance of differentiation in status among colleagues. The relationship between the exchange of knowledge and information and the differentiation in status, which sociologists have been so occupied with, can be interpreted as part of an internal marketing where the visibility of differences in competence and qualifications is the decisive factor.

In connection with new technology, the relationship between the organizational structure of the office and the impact of increased efficiency is of particular interest. According to Parkinson's law, an increase in working capacity in administration will make people find new tasks to exploit the new capacity. Technical changes in office environments have often had such consequences. Copying machines produce more copies, text processing machines produce more transcriptions and computer-based accounting systems provide more detailed accounting data, although there is no acknowledged need for this output. This type of economic adjustment is probably more common than we seem to think, and is typical of activity which is not organized in such a way that 'extra' working capacity results in reduced costs. A family is an example of an organization which does not have that quality, and reflections on a family-based economy (Kerblay, 1971) show adjustment mechanisms which resemble Parkinson's theory about the correlation between capacity and tasks in executive work.

The traditional office organization has a normative foundation which makes it hard to dismiss confidential members of the staff from a profit motive. The relationship between the clerk and the employer has not been determined by profit in the same way as with the production worker. Those who perform office work consult their surroundings to obtain various services necessary to fulfil their tasks. After some time, the demand for such services will become 'price elastic', and since technical and organizational changes usually come about through gradual evolution, attempts at increasing productivity will result in an unintentional growth in tasks.

Apart from the orientation toward internal labour markets and specific qualifications, there are other organizational characteristics specific to office environments. The development in the office sector has resulted in an accentuation of these features, and a description of the traditional clerk will to a diminishing degree reflect the organization of modern office work. First of all, general office work has largely been taken over by women. Male and female clerks have rarely competed on equal terms. Women have in different ways been outside the traditional pattern. Since women were first employed as office workers (about the time when the telephone and the typewriter were introduced), they have been assigned particular tasks. The lack of prescribed rules and standards for the evaluation of competence has given rise to differential treatment. Typical features of female office workers' occupational careers has put them in an unfavourable position in a competition where seniority was decisive and served as justification for differential treatment.

The jobs of female office workers vary considerably both in terms of content and qualifications. On the one hand, some secretaries are not highly specialized and need a spectrum of qualifications that are specific to the enterprise. On the other hand, there are specialized operators whose qualifications are connected with the operation of particular machines, rather than the enterprise in general. They may be compared to semi-skilled workers in the manufacturing industries. Both Mills and Lockwood show that office machine operators have mainly been women. Data processing represents a change in that respect. This technology involves great investment and costs. The equipment has, at least up to now, been expensive and has required further development by experts to be of use. Experts in EDP in many ways represent a technical elite in the office environment and a majority of them are men. In line with office tradition, data preparation and recording, which represents the tedious routine work in EDP, was primarily done by women.

Secondly, office environments have undergone a transformation, owing to a bureaucratization and professionalization of office jobs. The distribution of responsibility, promotion and salaries is determined by prescribed rules and administrative skills have been formalized into theoretical disciplines. It has become increasingly common to demand higher education for various office jobs.

The development of bureaucracies and professions has shown different characteristics in the various sections of the office. This reflects institutional conditions, among other things: in public administration, an organization based on prescribed rules is more common than in the private sector.

All these features have contributed to considerable changes in the way office work is organized. It is, however, difficult to determine the extent of these changes and their characteristics. In some fields the tendencies are obvious, whereas in other fields they are obscure. The demands for formal education are about to disrupt the established career pattern in offices and management. Unlike the young male trainee employed in an office in the 1930s, today's female assistant clerk has few opportunities to progress to responsible positions through internal labour markets.

On the other hand, there are indications that general office work is still based on qualifications specific to the enterprise. There is also a relatively low percentage of jobs where other kinds of qualifications are required, for example machine operators. Investigations of the relationship between the performance of practical office work and the occupational knowledge demanded show that company-specific knowledge is still a prerequisite of most office work. In a discussion of the potential for automation in office work, Lockwood quotes a statement from 1956 claiming that these possibilities are:

> Extremely limited by the simple fact that, although some people would deny it, the clerk often has to think for himself, is constantly meeting new sets of circumstances and his raw material is information. No electronic device has yet been designed which will read a letter written by a member of the public, realize what the letter is about and start off the necessary chain of actions required to answer it. (Lockwood, 1958, p. 94.)

Studies from the past few years indicate that this statement is still valid. Today office work is to a large extent based on comprehension and knowledge, thus restricting the possibilities for automating office systems. In an article concerning data processing systems, Vyssotsky writes as follows:

> Much clerical work, most of the work of such professionals as engineers and accountants, and some of the work of managers, consists of the applications of specific factual knowledge, gained through education and experience. It almost always turns out that nobody knows, in detail, what a particular knowledge worker does. The worker's supervisor can usually make a pretty clear statement on the subject, but one can often discover by watching for a few hours that the actual job function involves aspects that the supervisor did not state and does not normally think about. The worker is in no position to offer a complete description of how all possible combinations of circumstances are handled, the worker simply takes them as they come. (Vyssotsky, 1980, p. 23.)

Other empirical investigations of practical office work performance show the same results (Newmann, 1979; Wynn 1979). This knowledge structure creates several difficulties when it comes to the use of computer-based information systems. As Vyssotsky states, it has often appeared that nobody in an office organization really knows how the office actually operates. Although there are formal instructions which describe tasks and routines in detail, these give a poor description of how office work is performed in practice. The organization of office work is, to a large extent, implicitly defined in the practical knowledge of the various office workers. Yet nobody can fully explain how the work is actually carried out. Bitter experience has made DP experts aware of this. Describing the actual work pattern is one of the major problems of the development of efficient data processing systems. On many occasions, the only way is to involve in new developments everybody who implicitly knows how the work is actually accomplished. As a result, the development process becomes a process of learning and decision-making which is complex as well as expensive.

However, the description of the actual working process is only one part of the problem. In addition to involving an organized use of knowledge, the office also involves an organized production of knowledge. This aspect of organization and occupational knowledge in modern offices, has been dealt with in Wynn's investigation of informal conversation in office environments. Her cardinal statement is: 'In an office as it presently operates, the knowledge which is both means and product is dependent on interaction between people for its quality, relevance and appropriateness. These interactions are in turn dependent on social practices' (Wynn, 1979, p. 165).

Wynn's analysis shows that informal aspects of office work contribute to pattern of information processing which constitute the environment of the office. Within this pattern, practical knowledge evolves and is at the same time integrated into the existing common knowledge. Office work consists of a common practical understanding, which helps create and keep up to date the knowledge of the office employees. Wynn concludes, as Lockwood did twenty years earlier, that the particular organization of practical knowledge which office work represents, limits the possibility of standardization and specialization in the handling of information in office work.

2.3 Resistance to change — interests and power

The last statement to be elaborated is that changes within the office sector have met more powerful opposition than expected. People oppose reorganization and technical changes in various ways, ranging from lack of enthusiasm, support and understanding to active attempts to resist scheduled changes. Let us assume that opposition to change is due to a more or less rational belief that actual interests are threatened, and that opposition to change in office environments therefore is conditioned by the structure of actual interests in these environments.

What is the relation between organizational structure and the structure of interests in administrative units? According to Stinchcombe (1978), there are a variety of interests which are connected with the existing organization of an administration. First of all, an organization represents a distribution of possibilities of promotion. A reorganization would affect people's interests by altering these possibilities. Moreover, an organization represents a distribution of status, determined by the importance attached to different tasks and areas of responsibility. A reorganization may influence this distribution, thus affecting interests tied to status.

Administrative work consists of tying information to decisions. Stinchcombe states that the right to make a decision may be considered as a property right because different decisions benefit different persons. In order to reorganize administrative processes, one often has to interfere with conditions which have the characteristics of a property right.

The particular organization of an administrative unit corresponds to a certain structure of interests. There interests relate to possibilities of better payment, the value of various qualifications, and opportunities to influence decisions. In administrative work there is little difference between the structure of such interests and the organization of work, and this makes it difficult to separate the resolution of conflicts from the reorganization.

Therefore, reorganization will usually be met with various forms of opposition. Stinchcombe distinguishes between various types of reorganization according to their degree of interference with the structure of interests and the extent and nature of the opposition. The least complicated change is to increase the efficiency of communication within established patterns of status. The resistance to such reorganization is normally expressed through poor cooperation and frustration. The most difficult types of reorganization are those where the rights to make decisions are interfered with. In order to redistribute formal or informal property rights, the privileges often have to be bought, or at least compensated, thus increasing the costs of reorganization.

An administrative reorganization depends on the ability to mobilize enough power to fight the opposition, rather than to deal with technical questions. Stinchcombe underlines certain features of the relationship between the structure of decision-making in the organizations and characteristics of reorganization which will affect the prospects of accomplishing the change. Possibilities of mobilization of power will depend on pressure from the environment, the power structure of the organization, support from the central management, and the ability to bear the costs and to mobilize support for common values in the environment. Administrative reorganizations are political processes, not technical changes.

However, Stinchcombe does not discuss all aspects of the introduction of new techniques in management and office work. Another way of adopting new technology is to establish new organizations. Within production, this is probably the most common method of introducing new technology. But in management and office work one rarely starts from the beginning. Although technical changes are completed by the adaptation of an existing organization to technological innovations, any resistance to technical changes will depend on the structure of the organization and the interests of the members. Some organizations will apply new techniques in a way that does not require extensive changes and consequently avoids opposition. In other organizations, technical changes are directly connected with reorganizations which provoke conflicts. The choice of reorganization, the opposition to reorganization, and the ability to overcome opposition, will depend on the structure of the organization. Investigations have show that centralized organizations have a tendency to make reorganizations which evoke resistance, whereas decentralized organizations to a larger degree adjust to new technology in a less controversial manner. In decantralized organizations the distribution of power and competence along with a general openness to demands from the environments will encourage lower levels in the organizations to take an initiative to adapt to changed demands from the environment and technological development. There is less room for that in centralized organizations. However, in centralized organizations there is a power structure which makes it possible to overcome resistance to a reorganization which has been decided centrally, something which would be difficult to achieve in a decentralized organization.

Much of the literature about strategies for office automation deals with the choice between radical changes and gradual changes. In summary, the following are possible successful strategies for the introduction of new office technology.

The establishing of new organizational units, will probably be the most efficient way of introducing new technology. But there are limited opportunites to make use of this strategy, which can only be employed in special cases.

Radical changes will meet oppostion, and will therefore be difficult to carry through. In addition to general difficulties attached to radical changes in administration, it could be a complicated task to establish wholesale reorganiz-ations which fully exploit the new technology. This could increase the possibility of effective resistance.

What is left, is a decentralized and gradual change. Most people who have described strategies for office automation, recommend a moderate line of development. Although such strategies may increase the adaptability of office environments, the use of these methods will involve several problems in cases where extensive changes are expected, like office automation.

The first question is how to plan and coordinate the decentralized processes of development. We will see that many of the benefits of new technology rely on the integration of processes, tasks, and routines which, technically speaking, today are often performed discretely. Such integration can hardly take place without a superior and central decision-making process, which may clash with the decentralized activity.

The second question is how gradual change can result in a radical change. The choice of a gradual, deccentralized strategy involves the risk that old habits are easily transferred to the new organization. Thereby the office organization is subject to a limited increase in efficiency as regards existing routines, rather than a radical change.

3 THE DEVELOPMENT OF NEW OFFICE TECHNOLOGY

Most descriptions of future office technology are based on anticipated develop-ment of computer hardware. We assume that the price of electronics used in computers will continue to decrease, going down dramatically as compared with rising costs elsewhere. A microprocessor and a memory of 10 000 characters will become cheaper than the keys on a cash register or an electric typewriter. The ratio of output to price of conventional processing power will be improved by a factor of one hundred in the course of the next twenty years. The ratio of output to price on equipment for data entry and storage, transmission and presentation will be improved in relation to the general price trend, but not to the same extent as electronics. Moreover, new techniques and equipment will open up the employment of computer-based information technology for the processing of information which is represented by other means than characters or text, for example by speech or graphics. Generally, this implies that a series of financial and technical limitations on the application of computer-based information systems to office work will be reduced considerably.

These tendencies have been apparent for years. During the 1970s a series of new systems for administration and office work were developed. There are terminals for on-line data processing within an individual office. There are new types of equipment and systems which provide information in the form of text. Experiments have been carried out with a variety of new systems for the transmission of information in various forms, both within and between enterprises and organizations.

At present, a series of new techniques for office work are being developed: methods of optical character recognition and digital facsimile are being developed to the recording of text and graphics. New methods for the storage of digitized speech are being tested and new printers in the form of 'smart' copying machines are now on the market, as are split screens which can show more than one display of data and text at the same time.

Future office technology is foreseen as an extension of developments along these lines. Data and text processing systems will be connected with, and further integrated into, systems for the processing and transmission of information in other forms. Equipment and access to computers will become available to a wide variety of office environments at the same time as different systems and equipment are connected to form general electronically integrated information systems for office work.

However, much of this belongs to the future. Parts of the future office systems exist, but many problems of a technical, functional and organizational nature still remain. As in the 1950s, the introduction of this new and in many ways unfamiliar office technology is termed office automation, although it is difficult to have a clear idea of what is going to be produced automatically.

Today new office technology, as systematic knowledge of methods and principles of organization, gives the impression of being very comprehensive, vague and incomplete. It includes various techniques and types of technology which previously were discrete. There are dissimilar or partly contradictory opinions and theories about many of these issues. There are various ways of exploiting computer-based information technology to make office work more efficient. Which method will be used depends partly on how the production of knowledge in the form of equipment, systems, and actual work patterns is organized.

3.1 Product strategies

The major equipment and systems suppliers are the most important producers of knowledge about office techniques. In this field, today's situation is marked by confrontation between industries that never competed earlier. Giant corporations like IBM, Xerox and Bell are, on the basis of their own capacity and products, trying to explain as well as solve office problems by means of 'office automation'. Competing theories about office work and office technology are marketed along with competing products. Consequently there is today a variety of equipment and systems based on widely different conceptions of what is needed to otbain efficiency in office work. There are sophisticated terminal systems developed as an aid to knowledge-based work, as well as systems which have no benefits other than saving labour through traditional rationalization.

Falling prices of equipment will influence the development of new products. The suppliers are already facing the problem that prices are so low that equipment cannot be sold in the same way as computers were sold earlier. Text processing equipment at a price of £6000 cannot be sold in the same way as computer systems at £1.5 million.

Up to now, office technology has been brought to the market and sold as a combination of various products, such as machines, programs, training, service, and consultancy. The price trend has disturbed this pattern, although it is difficult to predict what consequences this may have for the development and distribution of new office techniques.

A third factor which will influence the development of new products is the rapid process of change. With a view towards present and future changes, it will be unfavourable to make choices and buy equipment that tie up capital and other resources of the enterprise for long periods. Developments favour purchases based on short-term needs. This justifies a choice of equipment which is inexpensive and demands limited changes in organization and a brief adjustment and transition period.

There are chiefly two product strategies for minimizing changes in organization and the time for adjustment and transition. Both strategies facilitate the integration of new systems and organizational arrangements with existing knowledge and routines. One strategy aims at developing programming tools which enable the individual employee to program the equipment himself. Another aims at developing systems which actually replace existing equipment and techniques, and at the same time open up further possibilities, for subsequent integration. By means of such systems, office routines can be made more efficient without creating particular demands for increased knowledge and changed routines (e.g. text processing systems, dedicated accounting systems, telephone and telex systems).

It is difficult to predict which strategy will prove to be the most profitable, and thereby the most successful, from the manufacturers' point of view. But one thing is certain, equipment will get cheaper, thus leading to increased flexibility. Moreover, it is highly likely that new office technology will require types of expertise in the organizations that are going to employ it that were not required earlier.

3.2 Introduction strategies

The final proving of new office technology will take place in those offices which are goint to employ such technology. This includes knowledge of tested techniques and established organizational arrangments. The situation among users is in many ways parallel to that of the manufacturers. Within larger administrative environments there will be departments for administrative rationalization or office rationalization and data processing. Demands from trade unions that decisions should be made through negotiations, will lead to stronger involvement by the personnel department. The various departments will have different opinions about how to achieve greater efficiency and employ dissimilar methods to carry through changes in working methods and organization. There has been and still is considerable disagreement concerning the definition of objectives and the distribution of responsibility and authority within the organizations, in connection with the introduction of new office technology. One example is text processing systems which are being introduced both as data processing systems and as traditional office equipment.

The drop in the price of equipment makes it increasingly difficult to justify the initial expense of the data processing systems introduced up to now. Reports and preliminary studies may easily involve equally high costs as buying or leasing equipment to experiment and learn how to take advantage of new techniques. When it comes to preliminary work, decision-making and systems design, the fall in the price of equipment will result in attempts to establish procedures which are less expensive and require less competence. The financial risk of purchasing equipment is now out of proportion to the cost of ensuring full use of the equipment. Therefore, less expensive and more adaptive methods of development and implementation will be preferred.

The rapid changes make new demands on the user organizations. Today it is impossible to introduce the electronic office through a clearly set out and planned reorganization. The transition period must be more 'evolutionary', proceeding as a series of smaller steps, where implications are still uncertain. The transition to new technology must be regarded as decisions or choices made at a stage where both present and future technology is partly unknown to the participants in the decision-making process. There is potentially a wide range of interpretations of technological issues, and various interpretations will be attached to different interests in the office environments. Such a situation may easily lead to decisions concerning the introduction of new technology being more or less accidental combinations of problems and solutions (March and Olsen, 1976). The introduction of text processing systems has in many cases taken such an erratic course (Pape, 1981). Rationalization experts and systems designers have warned strongly against this form of 'electronic happening' (Jardevall and Lovén, 1980). There are, however, few reasons to moralize on the fact that the development of office techniques does not meet the standards of rational planning. The problem is, in fact, that the conditions for such planning, in the form of well-defined objectives and well-known methods to achieve these objectives, are non-existent. The problem is to produce new objectives and new knowledge. In such a situation, the possibility to reverse the relationship between decisions, objects and means represents a possibility for innovations (March, 1971). The decisions must be viewed in the light of the development of knowledge in the organization.

On the part both of the manufacturer and the user, there are tendencies pointing towards gradual and decentralized strategies of change. Decentralization has in various discussions been placed among the 'soft values' which are contrasted with 'hard values' such as efficiency and productivity. Therefore one should perhaps stress that efficiency is the motive of decentralized strategies of change. Increase in efficiency depends on many factors. Decentralization will increase the organizations' capacity for learning and is a way of mobilizing sufficient knowledge for the extremely complicated decision-making process which the introduction of new office systems will involve. At the same time, decentralization is essential to make individual decisions in this process less complex.

On the basis of institutional theory, Strassman has argued that centralized systems design will result in a development governed by bureaucracy, which rarely contributes to systems that promote productivity. To increase productivity in information processing, systems design has to be subject to market forces, which implies that decision-making is moved from the centre of the organization to the parts closest to the market (Strassman, 1977, 1980).

However, such decentralization is a far from easy task. The delegation of power is always a process which involves conflict. In many instances the power structure of the organization will hamper the process of decentralization. But the power structure is not the only problem. The problem is rooted in the relationship between central or integrating mechanisms and local decisions. Hitherto the development of data processing systems has been marked by central decisions being made first, and subsequently influencing local decisions. What might encourage decentralization is the development of systems which do not need to be integrated until local arrangements and applications have been established.

The development of network-based systems inspire hope that this can be achieved. Such systems will provide an open framework for data communication supporting the integration of local applications. In various places, attempts are made at integrating office systems by means of the communication network of the organizations. Although a series of problems remain to be solved, until such systems have taken a simple and useful form, there are reasons, both technical and organizational, to believe that this approach leads to flexible and functional office systems.

4 DATA TECHNOLOGY AND THE OFFICE OF THE FUTURE – A SUMMARY

This article discusses various aspects of office work and office technology in a wide social perspective. Organizational as well as functional aspects of office work have been viewed in light of structural features of office surroundings. A central issue is the discussion of functional demands of the environment in relation to the potential use of computer-based information systems in office work. There are indications of frequent discord between these functional demands and demands arising from use of office technology.

In our discussion we have suggested two possible solutions to this conflict. Firstly increased flexibility in the technical as well as the financial sense, will afford better opportunities to make use of new technology for working methods which support knowledge-based office work: systems can be devised as an aid to information processing. Such applications have as their objective increased efficiency in the office rather than to reduce the need for labour. The process could be based on a local approach to the problem and local job information. Such a decentralized, gradual development, governed by efficiency, will provide opportunities to design systems and organization structures which will increase the flexibility of office work as well as efficiency.

The other possibility involves a reorganization of the relationship between organizations. By structuring external information – whether it concerns an order of goods which is to be executed, or the application of a law – in such a manner that it may be directly linked to internal computer-based routines, large areas of information processing can be automated. Such a development is likely to be based on cooperation between various enterprises or on political decisions. In fields like banking, tourism and the commodity trade the development of computer applications which directly influence competition and cooperation between enterprises is well under way.

When combining these two trends, we are presented with the following picture of future employment of computer-based information technology. The flow of information between enterprises and organizations will to an increasing degree be restructured and linked with computer-based information and communication systems. The prospects of automating the handling of such information are good. Along with new measures of cooperation and new contractual arrangements between organizations, systems will be developed for computer-based processing or organized routine information. Office work will still be based on knowledge of local and special conditions. However, computer-based remedies will be used in this work to an increasing degree because an increasing amount of external information is linked to such systems and because of the improved possibilities to make use of computerized solutions to local remedies.

In the introduction to this article, scepticism was expressed at the assertion that new information technology will result in dramatic changes in employment and working conditions in the office sector. History shows that new information technology along with changes in market conditions and the development of new organizational arrangements have led to growth in the office sector. The development of information technology and office work has been related to changes in the decision-making processes and the power structure in society. From an organizational sociological description of the developments in the office sector, our conclusion is that the employment of new technology in future office work must be viewed in relation to the future organization of information in more comprehensive social systems like markets and political/ administrative systems.

It is difficult to predict what consequences an extended use of technology in office work may involve. In the first place, this process will take place over a long period. In the user environment the ability to learn and to readjust will be a great importance. On higher organizational and social levels, the development requires a series of difficult judgements of interests and political decisions to be made. Moreover, there are various mechanisms which will work against rationalization within the office sector. A gradually decentralized organizational development will lead to an increasing use of office services that are easily accessible. The reorganization of markets and the relationship between organizations will result in counter-moves from competitors, the authorities and the organizations themselves. Such counter-moves could involve administrative costs.

But this must not lead us to believe that new technology does not provide opportunities for traditional means of rationalization of office work. There is every indication that new technology does, and that most of these possibilities have not been fully exploited. The slow development in the office sector today has probably resulted in a disparity between actual use of technology and the development of proven and efficient systems and techniques. Therefore it is not unlikely that the important trend in the years to come will be a wider distribution of applications which are well-known and proved — and that the first part of the 1980s will be characterized by already well-known systems and techniques rather than by office systems of the future.

REFERENCES

APEX (1979) *Office technology, the trade union response,* APEX, London.

Bird, E. (1980) *Information technology in the office: The impact on womens' jobs,* Equal Opportunities Commission, Manchester.

Braverman, H. (1974) *Work and Monopoly Capital,* Monthly Review Press, New York and London.

Doeringer, P. B., and Piore, M. J. (1971) *Internal Labour Markets and Manpower Analysis,* Lexington, Mass.

Elliot, (1977) The growth of whitecollar employment in Great Britain 1951 to 1971. *British Journal of Industrial relations,* **XV** 39—44.

Haider, K. (1979) Integrating Administrative Support towards the Automated Office. Proceedings of the Infotech State of the Art Conference. *New Frontiers in Office Automation,* Vienna, April 1979.

Jardevall, L., and Lovén, B. (1980) 80-tallets kontor — en elektronisk happening eller rationell planering (The office in the 1980s — an electronic happening or rational planning), *Nordata Conference 1980* (in Swedish).

Kerblay, B. (1971) Chayanov and the theory of peasantry as a specific type of economy, in Shanin, T. (ed.), *Peasants and Peasant Societies,* Penguin, Hamandsworth.

Kling, R. (1980) Social analysis of computing: theoretical perspectives in recent empirical research, *ACM-Computing Surveys,* **12**, 1.

Likestillingsrådet (1977) *Utviklingen i kvinners og menns stilling på kontor i 20-årsperioden 1956–76* (The change in male and female office workers situation during 1956–76), Oslo (in Norwegian).

Lockwood, D. (1958) *The Blackcoated Worker,* Allen & Unwin, London.

March, J. G. (1971) The technology of foolishness, *Civiløkonomen,* May 1971.

March, J. G., and Olsen, J. P. (1976) *Ambiguity and Choice in Organizations,* Universitetsforlaget, Bergen.

Mills, C. W. (1951) *White Collar,* Oxford University Press, New York.

Newmann, W. (1979) Information processing models of the office. Proceedings of the Infotech State of the Art Conference, *New Frontiers in Office Automation,* Vienna, April.

Newmann, W. (1980) Office models and office system design, in N. Naffah (ed.), *Integrated Office Systems – Burotics,* North-Holland, Amsterdam.

Newman, J. C., and Ward, T. B., (1980) Organisational Context of Office Systems, in N. Naffah (ed.), *Integrated Office Systems – Burotics,* North-Holland, Amsterdam.

Nora, S., and Minc, A. (1978) *L'informatisation de la Société,* Documentation Francaise, Paris.

Norsk Produktivitetsinstitutt (1981) *Å arbeide påkontor. En undersøkelse av miljø og arbeidsoppgaver,* (Office work. A study of tasks and working environment), NPI-rapport nr. 1110 (in Norwegian).

Pape, A. (1981) *Elektronisk tekstbehandling og arbeidsmiljø på kontor* (Electronic text processing and workers environment in offices), Norwegian Computing Centre, Oslo (in Norwegian).

Simon, H. A. (1976) *The new Science of Management Decision-making,* Prentice-Hall, Englewood Cliffs, N. J.

Stinchcombe, A. (1978) *On social factors in administrative innovations,* Arbeids-notat NAVF's senter for forskerutdanning, Oslo.

Strassman, P. A. (1977) Organizational productivity – the role of information technology, in B. Gilchrist (ed.), *Information Processing 1977,* North-Holland, Amsterdam.

Strassman, P. A. (1980) The office of the future: information management for the new age, *Technology Review* January 1980.

Vyssotsky, V. A. (1980) Computer systems: more evolution than revolution, *Journal of Systems Management,* February 1980.

Williamson, O. E. (1975) *Markets and Hierarchies: Analysis and Antitrust implications,* Free Press, New York.

Wynn, E. R. (1979) *Office Conversion as an Information Medium.* Ph. D. Dissertation, Department of Anthropology, University of California, Berkeley.

Index